MLA Handbook for Writers of Research Papers

Third Edition

Joseph Gibaldi
Walter S. Achtert

The Modern Language Association of America
New York 1988

Library of Congress Cataloging-in-Publication Data

Gibaldi, Joseph, 1942–
MLA handbook for writers of research papers.

Includes bibliographies and index.
1. Report writing—Handbooks, manuals, etc.
2. Research—Handbooks, manuals, etc. I. Achtert, Walter S.
II. Modern Language Association of America. III. Title.
LB2369.G53 1988 808′.02 88-5195
ISBN 0-87352-379-2

Cover design by Michael Soha.

Published by The Modern Language Association of America
10 Astor Place, New York, New York 10003-6981

Fourth printing, 1991

Printed on recycled paper.

CONTENTS

PREFACE FOR THE INSTRUCTOR

For nearly half a century, the style recommended by the Modern Language Association of America for scholarly manuscripts and student research papers has been widely adopted not only by journals and university presses but also by graduate schools, college departments, and individual instructors. The *MLA Handbook for Writers of Research Papers*, incorporating MLA style guidelines, serves as a supplementary text in writing courses or as a reference book for students to use independently. The extraordinary publication success of the first two editions of the *Handbook* throughout the United States, Canada, and other countries (Japanese translations appeared in 1980 and 1984) testifies to the continuing need for such a teaching and research tool.

This new edition has given us the opportunity to incorporate suggestions received from instructors who have been using the *Handbook* for a decade or more. In our revision, we have tried to clarify any ambiguities, to amplify matters only touched on previously, and to offer additional, and updated, examples when needed. We include more detail on the ways that computer technology can assist students in preparing research papers, and we fully cover the problem of documenting nonprint sources (films, television programs, recordings, performances, computer software, information from a computer service). Once again, to help students with spacing and indentation, we reproduce examples in typescript.

For the instructor who wishes to use the *MLA Handbook* as a class text, chapter 1 provides an expanded discussion of research and writing procedures: approaching the research paper, selecting a topic, using the library, compiling a working bibliography, taking notes, avoiding plagiarism, outlining, and writing the paper. This edition, like its predecessors, has chapters on the mechanics of writing (spelling, punctuation, names of persons, numbers, titles in the text, and quotations), on the format of the research paper (typing, paper, margins, spacing), and on abbreviations and reference words. The chapters "Preparing the List of Works Cited" and "Documenting Sources" contain comprehensive instructions on the MLA documentation style. (For the convenience of instructors who prefer a different system, we also explain alternative methods of citation.)

Aimed specifically at writers of research papers, the *MLA Handbook* pays only minimal attention to the problems that these writers share with all other writers. Questions of usage and writing style have been left, for the most part, to the many excellent manuals in that field.

Similarly, we have again resisted the temptation to include a complete research paper as an example, although we do provide a sample first page and a sample bibliography page at the end of the book, just before the comprehensive subject index. The response we have received from instructors suggests that their conceptions of the "ideal" research paper vary widely. Few teachers seem to agree on such basic questions as how the paper should be organized and developed, what its length should be, how many sources are necessary, and how much quotation and documentation it should include. Indeed, requirements often vary with different courses, assignments, and types of students. Many teachers report that they supply sample papers geared to specific classes and assignments or provide handouts offering supplementary comments on specific sections of the *Handbook*—for instance, relating the general discussion of research to the resources and services available in the school library, calling attention to material of particular relevance to the assignment, or stating the instructor's preferences on matters of form. We invite teachers who have found other helpful ways of using the *Handbook* in their classrooms to share this information with their colleagues.

Although it would be impossible to acknowledge everyone who assisted us with this project, we would like to express our gratitude to a number of persons who read and commented on drafts of the various editions of the *Handbook* and who offered us valuable advice and practical suggestions: John Algeo, Judith H. Altreuter, R. Neil Beshers, Richard Bjornson, Richard I. Brod, Frank N. Carney, Eric J. Carpenter, Gaetano Cipolla, Susan Y. Clawson, Thomas Clayton, Robert A. Colby, Claire Cook, Elizabeth W. Cowan, Gregory Cowan, Richard H. Cracroft, Marianna Davis, Robert J. Di Pietro, Richard J. Dunn, Bertie E. Fearing, John H. Fisher, Ron Fortune, Jesse Gatlin, Mary W. George, John C. Gerber, Dixie Goswami, Judy Goulding, Barbara Q. Gray, Martin Green, Stephen Greenblatt, Sterling Haig, Hilda Hanze, Laurel T. Hatvary, Carla Hayes, Carolyn G. Heilbrun, Kristin Helmers, Elizabeth Holland, Jeffrey Howitt, Robert R. Hoyt, Cheryl Hurley, Randall L. Jones, Joanne G. Kashdan, Weldon A. Kefauver, Gwin J. Kolb, Lawrence D. Kritzman, Barbara S. LaBarba, Richard A. LaFleur, Richard L. Larson, Sarah

N. Lawall, Linda J. Lehrer, William T. Lenehan, Bonnie Levy, Shirley Geok-Lin Lim, William A. Little, Richard Lloyd-Jones, Jane Marie Luecke, William D. Lutz, Sylvia Kasey Marks, Margaret McKenzie, Michael H. Means, Harrison T. Meserole, George J. Metcalf, Tess Midkiff, Susan P. Miller, James V. Mirollo, William G. Moulton, Neil E. Nakadate, Judith S. Neaman, Jasper P. Neel, John Neubauer, Stephen M. North, Mary Ann O'Donnell, Margaret C. Patterson, William H. Pell, Margot Rabiner, Nancy S. Rabinowitz, James L. Rolleston, Barbara Rotundo, Karen E. Rowe, Hans Rütimann, Marjorie L. Rütimann, Jeffrey L. Sammons, William D. Schaefer, Roslyn Schloss, Mina P. Shaughnessy, English Showalter, J. Kenneth Sieben, Carole G. Silver, Elaine S. Silver, Adeline Skillman, Gayatri Chakravorty Spivak, David Staines, William R. Streitberger, Madeleine B. Therrien, Vincent L. Tollers, Mario J. Valdés, Rebecca M. Valette, Renée Waldinger, Donald D. Walsh, Donna R. Walsh, Adrienne Marie Ward, Jerry W. Ward, Gerhard H. Weiss, Ray Werking, Jr., Thomas M. Wilcox, Katharina M. Wilson, Linda L. Wyman, Robert F. Yeager, Ella Mae York, R. B. Youngblood, and Ana Celia Zentella.

We would especially like to thank our current and former colleagues on the MLA staff for their unfailing support and help.

PREFACE FOR THE STUDENT

The *MLA Handbook for Writers of Research Papers* describes a set of conventions governing the written presentation of research. The recommendations on the mechanics and format of the research paper reflect the practices recommended by the Modern Language Association of America (a professional organization of some 25,000 instructors of English and other languages) and required by college teachers throughout the United States and Canada. Questions of writing style—choice of words, sentence structure, tone, and so on—are covered in other guides, such as those listed in section 1.11, and are not considered here.

Chapter 1 discusses the logical steps in research and writing—selecting a topic, using the library, preparing a working bibliography, taking notes, avoiding plagiarism, outlining, and writing drafts. Chapter 2 concerns the mechanics of writing (e.g., punctuation, spelling, capitalization, and the treatment of quotations and titles in the text), and chapter 3 deals with the formal preparation of the manuscript—typing (or, if you are using a word processor, printing) and binding the paper. Chapter 4, on preparing the list of works cited, provides well over two hundred examples illustrating bibliographic forms for both printed and other sources often referred to in research papers (e.g., films, recordings, and computer materials), and chapter 5 explains how to document such sources in the text. Following chapter 6, on abbreviations and reference words, the book concludes with sample pages from a research paper and a subject index.

The *MLA Handbook* is intended as both a classroom text and a reference tool. If you read it through first from cover to cover, you may find it easier to use later when you consult it for specific recommendations. The chapters are divided into numbered sections and subsections, and by citing these, rather than page numbers, the index makes it easy to find the information you need.

1. RESEARCH AND WRITING

1.1. The research paper

A research paper is, first and foremost, a form of written communication. Like other forms of nonfiction writing—letters, memos, reports, essays, articles, books—it should present information and ideas clearly and effectively. But when students are asked to write research papers, they often become so preoccupied with gathering material, taking notes, compiling bibliographies, and documenting sources that they forget to apply the knowledge and skills they have acquired through previous writing experiences. This discussion, therefore, begins with a brief review of the steps often outlined for expository writing. Although few writers follow such formal steps, keeping them in mind can suggest ways to proceed as you write:

If given a choice, select a subject that interests you and that you can treat within the assigned limits of time and space.

Determine your purpose in writing the paper. For example, do you want to describe something, explain something, argue for a certain point of view, or persuade your reader to think or do something?

Consider the type of audience you are writing for. For example, is your reader a specialist or a nonspecialist on the subject, someone likely to agree or disagree with you, someone likely to be interested or uninterested in the subject?

Develop a thesis statement expressing the central idea of your paper.

Gather your ideas and information in a preliminary list, eliminating anything that would weaken your paper.

Arrange materials in an order appropriate to the aims of the paper and decide on the method or methods you will use in developing your ideas (e.g., definition, classification, analysis, comparison and contrast, example).

Make a detailed outline to help you keep to your plan as you write.

Write a preliminary draft, making sure that you have a clear-cut introduction, body, and conclusion.

Read your preliminary draft critically and try to improve it, revising, rearranging, adding, and eliminating words, phrases, and sentences to make the writing more effective. Follow the same procedure with each subsequent draft.

Proofread the final draft, making all final corrections.

As you prepare and write research papers, always remember that no set of conventions for preparing a manuscript can replace lively and intelligent writing and that no amount of research and documentation can compensate for a poor presentation.

Although the research paper has much in common with other forms of writing, it differs from many of them in relying on sources of information other than the writer's personal knowledge and experience. It is based on primary research, secondary research, or a combination of the two. Primary research involves the study of a subject through firsthand observation and investigation, such as conducting a survey or carrying out a laboratory experiment; secondary research entails the examination of studies that others have made of the subject. Many academic papers, as well as many reports and proposals required in business, government, and other professions, depend on secondary research.

Research will increase your knowledge and understanding of a subject and will often lend authority to your ideas and opinions. The paper based on research is not a collection of other persons' thoughts and words but a carefully constructed presentation of ideas that relies on research sources for clarification and verification. While you must fully document the facts and opinions you draw from your research, the documentation should do no more than support your statements and provide concise information about the research cited; it should never overshadow the paper or distract the reader from the ideas you present.

1.2. Selecting a topic

All writing begins with a topic. If you have some freedom in choosing what to write about, look for a subject that interests you and that will maintain your interest throughout the various stages of research and writing. Some preliminary reading in the library will help you determine the extent of your interest. A library visit can also reveal whether enough serious work has been done on the subject to permit adequate research and whether the pertinent source materials are readily available.

In selecting a topic, keep in mind the time allotted to you and the expected length of the research paper. "Twentieth-Century World Politics" would obviously be too broad a subject for a ten-page term paper. Students commonly begin with fairly general topics and then refine them, by research and thought, into more specific ones. Here again, preliminary reading will be helpful. Consult books and articles as well as some general reference works, such as encyclopedias, and try to narrow your topic by focusing on a particular aspect or a particular approach. A student initially interested in writing on Shakespeare's imagery, for instance, might decide, after some careful thought and reading, to focus on the blood imagery in *Macbeth*; the topic "Modern Technology and Human Procreation" could likewise be narrowed to "The Future of Surrogate Motherhood."

Before beginning the project, make sure you understand the amount and depth of research required, the degree of subjectivity permitted, and the type of paper expected. Confer with your instructor if you need help in understanding the assignment or in choosing an appropriate topic.

1.3. Using the library

1.3.1. Introduction to the library

Since most of your research papers will draw on the works of experts and scholars, you should become thoroughly acquainted with the libraries to which you have access. Many academic libraries offer programs of orientation and instruction to meet the needs of all students, the beginning researcher as well as the graduate student. There may be introductory pamphlets or handbooks, guided tours, and lectures or even courses on using the library.

Nearly all public and academic libraries have desks staffed by professional reference librarians who can tell you about the available instructional programs and help you locate information. For a comprehensive introduction to the library, consult such books as Jean Key Gates, *Guide to the Use of Libraries and Information Sources* (5th ed., New York: McGraw, 1983), and Margaret G. Cook, *New Library Key* (3rd ed., New York: Wilson, 1975). Useful for reference works in literary studies are Margaret C. Patterson, *Literary Research Guide* (2nd ed., New York: MLA, 1983), and Nancy L. Baker, *A Research Guide for Undergraduate Students: English and American Literature* (2nd ed., New York: MLA, 1985).

1.3.2. The central catalog

The first step in getting to know your library is learning to use the central card catalog or, if the files are stored in a computer, the on-line catalog. Books are usually listed in the catalog by author, title, and subject. In some libraries, author cards, title cards, and subject cards are arranged alphabetically in a single catalog. Most libraries, however, divide the cards into two catalogs (author and title cards in one, subject cards in the other) or, more rarely, into three catalogs (one each for authors, titles, and subjects).

Next, become familiar with the two systems of classification most frequently used in American libraries: the Dewey decimal system and the Library of Congress system. The Dewey decimal system classifies books under 10 major headings:

000	General works
100	Philosophy
200	Religion
300	Social sciences
400	Language
500	Natural sciences
600	Technology and applied sciences
700	Fine arts
800	Literature
900	History and geography

The Library of Congress system divides books into 20 major groups:

A	General works
B	Philosophy and religion
C	General history
D	Foreign history
E–F	American history
G	Geography and anthropology
H	Social sciences
J	Political science
K	Law
L	Education
M	Music
N	Fine arts
P	Language and literature

Q Science
R Medicine
S Agriculture
T Technology
U Military science
V Naval science
Z Bibliography and library science

If you know the author of a book, you can locate it by consulting the author card. The combination of letters and numbers in the upper left-hand corner of the card (PS3521.A7255Z462 in the accompanying figure) is the designation by which the book is shelved in the library. The top few lines of the card contain the author's name and date of birth (Kauffmann, Stanley, 1916–), the full title of the book (*Albums of Early Life*), and complete publication information (published by Ticknor & Fields in the city of New Haven in the year 1980). The next few lines, in smaller print, describe the physical characteristics of the book (229 pages of text, 22 centimeters in height) and give the International Standard Book Number (0-89919-015-4). The lower half of the card shows the subject entries under which the book is also cataloged (Kauffmann, Stanley, 1916– —Biography; Authors, American—20th century—Biography; Critics—United States—Biography), the Library of Congress classification number (PS3521.A7255Z462), the Dewey decimal number (818'.5203), the alternative Dewey classification (B, for biography), and the Library of Congress catalog card number (80-14481).

PS3521
.A7255 **Kauffmann, Stanley, 1916-**
Z462 Albums of early life / Stanley Kauffmann. — New Haven : Ticknor & Fields, 1980.

229 p. ; 22 cm.

ISBN 0-89919-015-4

1. Kauffmann, Stanley, 1916- —Biography. 2. Authors, American—20th century—Biography. 3. Critics—United States—Biography. I. Title.

PS3521.A7255Z462 818'.5203 80-14481
[B] MARC

Library of Congress

If you know only the title of a book, you can locate it by consulting the title card, which differs from the author card only in that the title of the book appears at the top of the card.

Albums of early life

PS3521
.A7255 Kauffmann, Stanley, 1916-
Z462 Albums of early life / Stanley Kauffmann. — New Haven : Ticknor & Fields, 1980.

229 p. ; 22 cm.

ISBN 0-89919-015-4

1. Kauffmann, Stanley, 1916- —Biography. 2. Authors, American—20th century—Biography. 3. Critics—United States—Biography. I. Title,

PS3521.A7255Z462 818'.5203 80-14481
[B] MARC

Library of Congress

If you have no author or title in mind but wish to find a book or books on a particular topic, consult the subject card, which differs from the author card only in that the subject appears at the top of the card. (To find the appropriate headings, see *Library of Congress Subject Headings* or the list your library follows.)

Critics--United States--Biography

PS3521
.A7255 Kauffmann, Stanley, 1916-
Z462 Albums of early life / Stanley Kauffmann. — New Haven : Ticknor & Fields, 1980.

229 p. ; 22 cm.

ISBN 0-89919-015-4

1. Kauffmann, Stanley, 1916- —Biography. 2. Authors, American—20th century—Biography. 3. Critics—United States—Biography. I. Title.

PS3521.A7255Z462 818'.5203 80-14481
[B] MARC

Library of Congress

When using an online catalog, you can also locate books by author, title, and subject, but, instead of flipping through library cards and moving from one drawer to another, you conduct the search by typing appropriate information and commands on the keyboard of a computer terminal. If you enter the author's full name, the screen displays a list of all the books the library has by that author. When you select one that interests you, the screen shows the same bibliographic information for that book as a library card would. Entering the title produces a list of all the books the library has with that title. Again, when you select the appropriate one, the relevant bibliographic data appears. Entering a subject yields a list of books on that subject.

The online catalog can help you locate a book even if you lack some of the information you would ordinarily use for the search. If you know only the beginning part of the title—for example, only *Advertising, Competition*, instead of *Advertising, Competition, and Public Policy: A Simulation Study*—you can enter what you know, and the screen will display all titles that begin with those words. If you know only an author's last name, you can obtain a list of all authors with that last name. The computer-stored catalog will also allow you to initiate much more sophisticated searches. If, for instance, you know only a word in the middle of a title—let us say, using the above example, only *Competition*—you may call up a list of all titles containing that word. If you know only the publisher's name, you can usually get a list of that publisher's books by searching for the publisher's International Standard Book Number (ISBN) prefix.

Online catalog systems vary considerably in the assistance they offer. On command, some will even print out the bibliographic data displayed on the screen, thus not only saving you the time and effort of copying the information but also eliminating the possibility of transcription errors. Be sure to find out exactly what your library's system can do, and closely follow the directions for using it.

1.3.3. Reference works

Besides knowing how to locate books on specific subjects, you should know the range of general reference works available to you, such as dictionaries, encyclopedias, biographical works, yearbooks, atlases, and gazetteers. The following are among the most widely used:

Dictionaries

Oxford English Dictionary
Webster's Third New International Dictionary of the English Language

Encyclopedias

American Academic Encyclopedia
Collier's Encyclopedia
Columbia Encyclopedia
Encyclopedia Americana
Encyclopaedia Britannica

Biographical works for persons no longer living

Dictionary of American Biography (for the United States)
Dictionary of Canadian Biography
Dictionary of National Biography (for Great Britain)
Webster's Biographical Dictionary (also includes persons still living)

Biographical works for persons still living

Contemporary Authors
Current Biography
International Who's Who
Webster's Biographical Dictionary (also includes persons no longer living)
Who's Who in America

Yearbooks

Americana Annual
Britannica Book of the Year
Europa Year Book

Atlases

National Atlas of the United States of America
Times Atlas of the World

Gazetteers

Columbia-Lippincott Gazetteer of the World
Webster's New Geographical Dictionary

You should know, too, that all major fields of study have specialized dictionaries and encyclopedias, which are also useful sources for preliminary reading in a subject. The following are just a sampling:

Art

Encyclopedia of World Art
McGraw-Hill Dictionary of Art
Oxford Companion to Art

Astronomy

Cambridge Encyclopaedia of Astronomy
Larousse Encyclopedia of Astronomy

Biology

Dictionary of Biology
Encyclopedia of Bioethics
Encyclopedia of the Biological Sciences

Chemistry

Condensed Chemical Dictionary
Encyclopedia of Chemistry

Computer science

Computer Dictionary and Handbook
Encyclopedia of Computer Science

Dance

Concise Oxford Dictionary of Ballet
Encyclopedia of Dance and Ballet

Earth sciences

Cambridge Encyclopaedia of Earth Sciences
Encyclopedia of Earth Sciences

Economics

Encyclopedia of Economics
McGraw-Hill Dictionary of Modern Economics

Education

Encyclopedia of Education

Film

Dictionary of Films
International Encyclopedia of Film
Oxford Companion to Film

History

Dictionary of American History
Encyclopedia of World History

Law

Black's Law Dictionary
Encyclopedic Dictionary of International Law

Literature

Cassell's Encyclopaedia of World Literature
Oxford Companion to American Literature
Oxford Companion to Canadian Literature
Oxford Companion to Classical Literature
Oxford Companion to English Literature
Oxford Companion to French Literature
Oxford Companion to German Literature
Oxford Companion to Spanish Literature
Penguin Companion to American Literature
Penguin Companion to Classical, Oriental, and African Literature
Penguin Companion to English Literature
Penguin Companion to European Literature

Mathematics

Prentice-Hall Encyclopedia of Mathematics
Universal Encyclopedia of Mathematics

Medicine

Dorland's Medical Dictionary
Stein and Day International Medical Encyclopedia

Music

Harvard Dictionary of Music
New Grove Dictionary of Music and Musicians
Oxford Companion to Music

Philosophy

Dictionary of Philosophy
Encyclopedia of Philosophy

Physics

Encyclopaedic Dictionary of Physics
Encyclopedia of Physics

Psychology

Encyclopedia of Psychology

Religion

Encyclopaedia of Religion and Ethics
International Standard Bible Encyclopedia
Interpreter's Dictionary of the Bible

Science and technology

Harper Encyclopedia of Science
McGraw-Hill Encyclopedia of Science and Technology

Social sciences

Dictionary of Social Sciences
International Encyclopedia of the Social Sciences

1.3.4. Bibliographic sources

Articles in specialized reference works often provide brief bibliographies that can help in the early stages of research. To find more recent and other additional material on a subject, you can turn to indexes, bibliographies, and abstracts. The *New York Times Index* lists news stories and feature articles in that newspaper, and there are similar indexes (in printed, microform, or data-base formats) for many other newspapers in the United States, including the *Chicago Tribune*, *Christian Science Monitor*, *Los Angeles Times*, *New Orleans Times-Picayune*, *Wall Street Journal*, and *Washington Post*. The *National Newspaper Index* covers the *Christian Science Monitor*, *New York Times*, and *Wall Street Journal*. The *Canadian Newspaper Index* provides a subject and name index to Canada's leading newspapers.

The widely known and much used *Readers' Guide to Periodical Literature*, which began publication in 1900, indexes the contents of magazines. Microfilm by-products of computerized indexes, such as the *Magazine Index*, are available in many libraries and can provide easier and more up-to-date access to current literature. (For periodical literature published before 1900 or in other countries, consult the appropriate sources in your library.) Also useful is the *Essay and General Literature Index*, which lists essays and articles published in books. The *CBS News Index* offers microform transcripts of that network's daily television news broadcasts as well as other news programs, such as *60 Minutes* and *CBS Reports*. (See 1.3.6 for a discussion of microform.)

Just as the various subject areas have their own reference works, they also have specialized indexes, such as the following:

Art

Art Index

Biology

Biological and Agricultural Index

Business

Business Periodicals Index

Chemistry

Current Abstracts of Chemistry and Index Chemicus

Classical studies

L'année philologique

Education

Current Index to Journals in Education
Education Index

Engineering

Engineering Index Monthly and Author Index

Humanities

British Humanities Index
Humanities Index

Language and literature

MLA International Bibliography

Law

Index to Legal Periodicals

Medicine

Index Medicus

Music

Music Index

Philosophy

Philosopher's Index

Religion

Religion Index One: Periodicals

Science and technology

Applied Science and Technology Index
General Science Index
Science Citation Index

Social sciences

Social Sciences Index

Abstracting services provide useful summaries of the contents of journal articles. Among the many reference works of this type are the following:

Abstracts in Anthropology
Biological Abstracts
Chemical Abstracts
Historical Abstracts
Key to Economic Science
Language and Language Behavior Abstracts
Physics Abstracts
Psychological Abstracts
Religious and Theological Abstracts
RILA (art)
RILM (music)
Science Abstracts
Sociological Abstracts

Summaries of doctoral dissertations are available in *Dissertation Abstracts International* (entitled *Dissertation Abstracts* until 1969), which is divided into three series: A, the humanities and social sciences; B, the sciences; and C, European dissertations.

1.3.5. Location of library materials

Library books are kept either on open shelves, to which the public has direct access, or in closed stacks. To obtain a book in closed stacks you usually have to present a call slip to a library staff member, who will locate the book for you. Regardless of the system used, all libraries keep some books separate from the main collection. If a book is kept in a special area, the catalog card should show the location. For example, in some libraries an *f* preceding the call number on the card means "folio size" and shows that the book is shelved with oversized books. The word *Reserved* on a card indicates a book currently required in a course and stored in a special section, at the instructor's request, to keep it available for students in the course and, usually, to confine its use to the library. A book shelved in the reference section, designated by an *R* or *Ref.* on the catalog card, must also remain in the library. Some libraries have additional special collections, such as rare books or government documents, that are kept separate from the main collection.

Libraries also commonly set aside specific areas for various types of materials—current periodicals, pamphlets, clippings, and nonprint materials, like pictures, maps, films, slides, recordings, videotapes, audiotapes, and compact discs. Consult the library directory or the librarian for locations.

1.3.6. Other library resources and services

In addition to knowing about these print and nonprint materials, you should become familiar with microforms as well as with the resources provided by computer technology. *Microform* designates printed matter greatly reduced in size by microphotography; common types are microfilm, microcard, and microfiche. To use microforms, you need a special "reader" to magnify them. Library staff members are usually on hand specifically to assist researchers in locating microform materials and operating the readers.

Some academic libraries also provide computer terminals that have direct access to data bases. Many of the bibliographic sources listed in 1.3.4 are available in both data-base and print forms. Commercial vendors, such as Dialog, Wilsonline, Bibliographic Retrieval Services (BRS), and Systems Development Corporation (SDC), acquire such data bases and make them accessible to libraries. Because "online searching" involves substantial costs, many libraries limit this service to faculty members and advanced students and may also charge a fee for its use.

If your library permits you to do online searching, you will probably begin by conferring with a staff member who specializes in computer searches. In this meeting, the librarian will help you to identify the most useful data bases for your research and to translate your search into one or more "descriptors," words and names under which information is stored. You can then call up pertinent bibliographic references by communicating the appropriate descriptors to the computer, though it is often the librarian who actually conducts the search.

The list resulting from the computer search appears on the terminal's screen, but a printout is usually available as well. The list may be either printed out immediately at the terminal or, for a lower fee, mailed to you by the vendor. In addition, some distributors of data-base services, such as the Educational Resources Information Center (ERIC), have both an information-storage system and a document-delivery system—that is, they supply not only bibliographic references but also, at a much higher cost, copies of the documents themselves.

Students with their own computers equipped with modems can access online data bases on their own. An excellent and well-received guide for online research is Alfred Grossbrenner, *How to Look It Up Online* (New York: St. Martin's, 1987), which, directed to both the home user and the library user, covers a number of scholarly and educational data bases.

Although not all libraries provide computer assistance, most offer other services you should know about, such as copying facilities and interlibrary loans. If, for example, your library does not have the sources you need, ask whether it can borrow them from another library. If it can, consult the *National Union Catalog* to find out which libraries have the books you want or, if you need periodicals, the *Union List of Serials* and *New Serial Titles*. Most libraries have mutual agreements that make the exchange of research materials on a regional, state, or national level quick and inexpensive.

Obviously, the more you know about the library and the materials and services it provides, the more successful you will be in gathering information and ideas for your research paper.

1.4. Compiling a working bibliography

The first stage in research is discovering where to look for information and opinions on your topic. Begin by compiling a working bibliography—a list of books, articles, and other sources you want to examine. Your preliminary reading in both general and specialized reference works will probably provide the first titles for this list. You can add others by consulting appropriate subject headings in the library catalog and checking indexes and bibliographies, such as those mentioned in the preceding section. Also read carefully through the bibliography and notes of each book and article you consult; more often than not, your reading will lead you to additional important sources. Your working bibliography will frequently change during your research as you add new titles and eliminate those that do not prove useful and as you explore and emphasize some aspects of your subject in preference to others. The working bibliography will evolve into the final bibliography, the list of works cited that appears at the end of the research paper.

Many instructors recommend that students use index cards in compiling the working bibliography—one card for each source. Index cards allow much greater flexibility than does a continuous list on sheets of paper. For example, as you research, you can arrange and rearrange your sources however you wish (e.g., in alphabetical order, in chronological order by date of publication, or in order of relevance to your topic) and as often as you wish with little inconvenience; index cards also permit you to divide sources into groups (e.g., those already consulted and those not yet consulted, those most useful and those less so).

In adding sources to your working bibliography, write down all the publication information needed for the final bibliography. For a book, record the author's full name, the full title (including any subtitle), the edition (if it is a second or later edition), the number of the volume and the total number of volumes (if it is a multivolume work), the city of publication (note only the first city if several are listed), the publisher, and the year of publication. For an article in a newspaper or a magazine (see 4.7.1–2), include the author's name, the title of the article, the title of the periodical, the date of publication, and the inclusive page numbers of the article (i.e., the number of the page on which the article begins, a hyphen, and the number of the page on which the article ends). For an article in a scholarly journal (see 4.7.3), include the author's name, the title of the article, the title of the journal, the volume number, the year of publication, and the inclusive page numbers of the article. Recording all the information about your sources when you first consult them will save you time and spare you many last-minute problems. (See ch. 4 for complete information on compiling the final bibliography of the research paper.)

In addition, at the bottom of the index card note the exact source of the bibliographic information, in case you need to recheck the source or to borrow the material from another library (a library often requires a printed source for verification before it will accept a request for an interlibrary loan). Leave room, too, in the upper right-hand corner of the card, to record the call number or any other identifying information needed to locate the work.

Geherin, David. The American Private Eye: The Image in Fiction. New York: Ungar, 1985.

PS 374 D4 G39

'85 MLA Bib. 1:7414

The sample bibliography card above contains not only all the information needed for the final bibliography (author's name, full title, and relevant publication information) but also information useful in conducting research: at the bottom, the source of the reference (*1985 MLA International Bibliography*, vol. 1, item 7414) and, in the upper right-hand corner, the call number indicated for the book in the card catalog.

Once you have a reference in hand, verify the publication facts on your bibliography card and add any missing information that you will need for the final bibliography. For a book, check the author's name, title, subtitle (if any), edition (if relevant), the number of volumes, the city of publication, the publisher, and the year of publication. (This information normally appears on the title and copyright pages of the book.) For an article in a periodical, check the author's name, the title of the article, the title of the periodical, the date of publication, and the inclusive page numbers. If the article is in a scholarly journal, check the volume number as well. (Volume numbers and the dates of publication normally appear on the title pages of periodicals.) Correct any information on the bibliography card that does not match the data obtained from the work itself.

If compiled with care and attention, the working bibliography will be invaluable to you throughout the preparation of your paper. It will, on the one hand, function as an efficient tool for finding and acquiring information and ideas and, on the other, provide all the facts you will need for your final bibliography.

1.5. Taking notes

After you have verified the publication information for a source, the next step is to read and evaluate the material. You should not assume, of course, that something is truthful or trustworthy just because it is in print. Some material may be based on incorrect or outdated information, on poor logic, or on the author's own narrow opinions. Weigh what you read against your own knowledge and intelligence as well as against other treatments of the subject.

When you find material that you consider reliable and useful to your purpose, you will want to take notes on it. Although everyone agrees that note-taking is essential to research, probably no two researchers use exactly the same methods. Some take notes on a second set of index cards; others write in notebooks, beginning each new entry on a fresh page; still others favor loose-leaf or legal-size pages clipped together according to one system or another. Whatever your preference, take down first, at the very top of the page or card, the author's full name and the complete title of the source—enough information to enable you to locate the corresponding bibliography card easily when you need it.

There are, generally speaking, three methods of note-taking: summary, paraphrase, and quotation. Summarize if you want to record only the general idea of large amounts of material. If you require detailed notes on specific sentences and passages, but not the exact wording, you may wish to paraphrase—that is, to restate the material in your own words. But when you believe that some sentence or passage in its original wording might make an effective addition to your paper, transcribe that material exactly as it appears, word for word, comma for comma. Whenever you quote from a work, be sure to use quotation marks scrupulously in your notes to distinguish between verbatim quotation and summary or paraphrase. Keep an accurate record, preferably in the left-hand margin, of the page numbers of all material you summarize, paraphrase, or quote. When a quotation continues to another page, be careful to note where the page break occurs, since only a small portion of what you transcribe may ultimately find its way into your paper.

In taking notes, try to be both concise and thorough. Above all, however, strive for accuracy, not only in copying words for direct quotation but also in summarizing and paraphrasing authors' ideas. Careful note-taking will help you avoid the problem of plagiarism.

1.6. Plagiarism

You may have heard the word *plagiarism* used in relation to lawsuits in the publishing and recording industries. You may also have had classroom discussions about academic plagiarism. Plagiarism is the act of using another person's ideas or expressions in your writing without acknowledging the source. The word comes from the Latin word *plagiarius* ("kidnapper"), and Alexander Lindey defines it as "the false assumption of authorship: the wrongful act of taking the product of another person's mind, and presenting it as one's own" (*Plagiarism and Originality* [New York: Harper, 1952] 2). In short, to plagiarize is to give the impression that you have written or thought something that you have in fact borrowed from someone else.

Plagiarism in student writing is often unintentional, as when an elementary school pupil, assigned to do a report on a certain topic, goes home and copies down, word for word, everything on the subject in an encyclopedia. Unfortunately, some students continue to use such "research methods" in high school and even in college without realizing that these practices constitute plagiarism. You may certainly use other persons' words and thoughts in your research paper, but you must acknowledge the authors.

Plagiarism often carries severe penalties, ranging from failure in a course to expulsion from school.

The most blatant form of plagiarism is to repeat as your own someone else's sentences, more or less verbatim. Suppose, for example, that you want to use the material in the following passage, which appears on page 906 in volume 1 of the *Literary History of the United States*:

> The major concerns of Dickinson's poetry early and late, her "flood subjects," may be defined as the seasons and nature, death and a problematic afterlife, the kinds and phases of love, and poetry as the divine art.

If you write the following without any documentation, you have committed plagiarism:

```
The chief subjects of Emily Dickinson's poetry
include nature and the seasons, death and the
afterlife, the various types and stages of love,
and poetry itself as a divine art.
```

But you may present the information if you credit the authors:

```
Gibson and Williams suggest that the chief
subjects of Emily Dickinson's poetry include
nature, death, love, and poetry as a divine art
(906).
```

The sentence and the parenthetical documentation at the end indicate the source, since the authors' names and the volume and page numbers refer the reader to the corresponding entry in the bibliography:

Gibson, William M., and Stanley T. Williams. "Experiment in Poetry: Emily Dickinson and Sidney Lanier." <u>Literary History of the United States</u>. Ed. Robert E. Spiller et al. 4th ed. Vol. 1. New York: Macmillan, 1974. 899-916.

Other forms of plagiarism include repeating someone else's particularly apt phrase without appropriate acknowledgment, paraphrasing another person's argument as your own, and presenting another's line of thinking as though it were your own. Two more examples follow:

Original source

This, of course, raises the central question of this paper: What should we be doing? Research and training in the whole field of restructuring the world as an "ecotopia" (eco-, from *oikos*, household; -topia from *topos*, place, with implication of "eutopia"—"good place") will presumably be the goal. (From E. N. Anderson, Jr., "The Life and Culture of Ecotopia," *Reinventing Anthropology*, ed. Dell Hymes [1969; New York: Vintage-Random, 1974] 275.)

Plagiarized in student writing

Humankind should attempt to create what we might call an "ecotopia."

Original source

Humanity faces a quantum leap forward. It faces the deepest social upheaval and creative restructuring of all time. Without clearly recognizing it, we are engaged in building a remarkable civilization from the ground up. This is the meaning of the Third Wave.

Until now the human race has undergone two great waves of change, each one largely obliterating earlier cultures or civilizations and replacing them with ways of life inconceivable to those who came before. The First Wave of change—the agricultural revolution—took thousands of years to play itself out. The Second Wave—the rise of industrial civilization—took a mere hundred years. Today history is even more accelerative, and it is likely that the Third Wave will sweep across history and complete itself in a few decades. (From Alvin Toffler, *The Third Wave* [1980; New York: Bantam, 1981] 10.)

Plagiarized in student writing

There have been two revolutionary periods of change in history: the agricultural revolution and the industrial revolution. The agricultural revolution determined the course of history for thousands of years; the industrial civilization lasted about a century. We are now on the threshold of a new period of revolutionary change, but this one may last for only a few decades (10).

In the first example, the writer borrowed a specific term (*ecotopia*) without acknowledgment; in the second example, the writer presented another's line of thinking without giving that person credit. Once again, however, the students could have avoided the charge of plagiarism by rewording slightly and inserting appropriate parenthetical documentation.

Humankind should attempt to create what E. N. Anderson, Jr., has called an "ecotopia" (275).

According to Alvin Toffler, there have been two revolutionary periods of change in history: the agricultural revolution and the industrial revolution. The agricultural revolution determined the course of history for thousands of years; the industrial civilization lasted about a century. We are now on the threshold of a new period of revolutionary change, but this one may last for only a few decades (10).

As before, the parenthetical documentation in each revision identifies the source of the borrowed material and refers the reader to the full description of the work in the bibliography at the end of the paper:

Anderson, E. N., Jr. "The Life and Culture of Ecotopia." Reinventing Anthropology. Ed. Dell Hymes. 1969. New York: Vintage-Random, 1974. 264-81.

Toffler, Alvin. The Third Wave. 1980. New York: Bantam, 1981.

If you have any doubt about whether or not you are committing plagiarism, cite your source or sources.

1.7. Outlining

1.7.1. Working outline

Outlining is an important intermediate stage between research and writing. But you should not wait until you have completed your research to begin to draw up an outline. In fact, some instructors prefer that the outline evolve during the research stage. These instructors usually ask students at the very outset of the assignment to outline a tentative list of topics to research, and they suggest that this working or "scratch" outline be continually revised—topics dropped, added, modified—as the research progresses. Using a working outline will help you to keep track of all important aspects of your subject and to focus your research only on relevant topics. Continual revision of the working outline, moreover, will encourage you to change your thinking and your approach as new information modifies your understanding of the subject.

1.7.2. Thesis statement

When you have concluded your research for the paper, it is time to shape the information you have at hand into a unified, coherent whole. Begin by framing a thesis statement for your paper: a single sentence that formulates both your topic and your point of view toward it. Writing this statement is a way of making sure that you know where you are heading and that you remain on the right track as you plan and write. Since the experience of writing may alter your original plans, do not hesitate to refine the thesis statement as you write the paper. Many instructors require students to submit a thesis statement for approval some two or three weeks before the paper is due. If you have difficulty writing one, talk with your instructor about the research you have done and about what you want to say; given this information, your instructor can probably help you frame an appropriate thesis statement.

The following sample is a thesis statement for section 1.3.

```
Students who wish to write successful research
papers should know as much as possible about the
library.
```

1.7.3. Final outline

After you have a satisfactory thesis statement, the next step is to transform your working outline into a final outline for writing the paper. The final outline will help you organize your ideas and the accumulated research into a logical, fluent, and effective paper. Again, many instructors request that an outline be submitted either before or with the paper.

With your working outline as a starting point, carefully review all your notes for additional ideas and supporting references. Next, read over what you have written down and delete everything that is irrelevant to the thesis statement or that would weaken the paper. Eliminating material is often painful since it is only natural to want to use everything you have collected and to impress your readers (especially teacher-readers) with all the work you have done and with all you now know on the subject. But you should fight these tendencies, for the inclusion of unhelpful, misleading, irrelevant, or repetitive material will detract from the effectiveness of your paper. In short, keep your thesis statement and your audience in mind. Include only the ideas and information that will help you accomplish what you have set out to do and that will interest and inform your readers, not confuse or bore them.

As you continue to read, reread, and think about the ideas and information you have decided to use, you will begin to see connections between various items, and certain patterns of organization will suggest themselves. Bring related material together under general headings, and arrange these sections so that one logically flows into another. Then order the subjects under each heading so that they, too, logically flow from one into the other. Finally, plan an effective introduction and a conclusion appropriate to the sequence you have worked out. Common organizing principles are time (useful for historical discussions), space (useful for some descriptions), and logic. A logical development may move, for example, from the general to the specific (e.g., from the problems of transportation to the disadvantages of travel by automobile) or from the specific to the general (e.g., from the disadvantages of travel by automobile to the problems of transportation).

In choosing an organizational plan, keep in mind the method or methods you will use in developing your paper. For example, do you plan to define, classify, or analyze something? to use descriptive details or give examples? to compare or contrast one thing with another? The procedures you intend to adopt will obviously influence the way you arrange your material, and they should be evident in your outline.

In general, then, make your outline as detailed as possible. It is a good idea to indicate, specifically and precisely, not only the methods of development you will use but also the quotations and reference sources. All this planning will take a good deal of time and thought, and you may well make several preliminary outlines before you arrive at the one you will follow. But the time and thought will be well spent. The more planning you do, the easier and more efficient the writing will be.

If the final outline is only for your use, its form will have little importance. If it is to be submitted, your instructor will probably discuss the various forms of outline—for example, the topic outline (which uses only short phrases throughout) and the sentence outline—and tell you which to use. Whatever the form, however, maintain it consistently.

The descending parts of an outline are normally labeled in the following order:

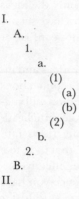

```
I.
  A.
    1.
      a.
        (1)
          (a)
          (b)
        (2)
      b.
    2.
  B.
II.
```

Logic requires that there be a *II* to complement a *I*, a *B* to complement an *A*, and so forth. The following sample is a topic outline of section 1.3.

```
            Using the Library
Introduction--the importance of the library for
the research paper
I.  Introduction to the library
    A.  Programs of orientation and instruction
        1.  Pamphlets, handbooks, other
            materials distributed by the
            library
        2.  Class visits, tours, lectures,
            courses
```

    B. Books about the library (examples: Gates, Cook, Patterson, Baker)
II. The central catalog
    A. Methods of locating books in the catalog
        1. Author
        2. Title
        3. Subject
    B. Methods of arranging cards
        1. Single catalog
        2. Two or more catalogs
    C. Systems of classification
        1. Dewey Decimal system
        2. Library of Congress system
    D. Sample catalog cards
        1. Author
        2. Title
        3. Subject
    E. Online catalog
III. Reference works
    A. General works (dictionaries, encyclopedias, biographical works, yearbooks, atlases, gazetteers)
    B. Specialized dictionaries and encyclopedias (in alphabetical order: art, astronomy, etc.)
IV. Bibliographic sources
    A. Indexes to periodicals (newspapers, magazines) and television news broadcasts

B. Specialized bibliographies and indexes (in alphabetical order: art, biology, etc.)

C. Abstracts (in alphabetical order: Abstracts in Anthropology, etc.)

V. Location of library materials

A. Main collection

1. Open shelves

2. Closed stacks

B. Special sections

1. Folio-size books

2. Reserved books

3. Reference works

4. Periodicals

5. Pamphlets, clippings, nonprint materials

VI. Other library resources and services

A. Microforms: microfilm, microcard, microfiche

B. Computer assistance in research

C. Other assistance (e.g., copying facilities, interlibrary loans)

Conclusion--the importance of knowing about the library, its materials and services

1.8. Writing drafts

Once you have your thesis statement and final outline, you are ready to begin writing. But do not expect your first draft to be the finished product. The successful research paper is usually the culmination of a series of drafts.

Start off by trying to set down all your ideas in the order in which you want them to appear. Even though the writing may be hasty and fairly rough, the first draft should attempt to follow your outline closely. You should then read over this raw material and try to refine it. Next, review the corrected draft and make further changes. Continue this process until you are satisfied that you have done the best you can in the time available.

In revising, you may add, eliminate, and rearrange material. If a section in the first draft seems unclear or sketchy, you may have to expand it by writing another sentence or two or even a new paragraph. Similarly, to improve the fluency and coherence of the paper, you may need to add transitions to show how one sentence relates to another or how one paragraph leads to the next. For the sake of unity and reader interest, you should delete any material that is irrelevant, unimportant, repetitive, or dull and dispensable. If the presentation of ideas seems illogical or confusing, you may find that you can clarify by rearranging phrases, clauses, sentences, or paragraphs.

In later drafts you should concern yourself with the more mechanical kinds of revision. For example, strive for more precise and economical wording. Try, in addition, to vary your sentence patterns as well as your choice of words. Finally, correct all technical errors, using a standard writing guide to check punctuation, grammar, and usage and consulting a standard dictionary to check the spelling and meaning of words. Your last draft, retyped, carefully proofread, and corrected, is the text of your research paper.

1.9. Using a word processor in preparing research papers

Because of the many stages involved in preparing research papers and the need for revision at many of those stages, word processors, with their storage, retrieval, file-merging, and editing capabilities, are particularly useful for research writing.

With a word processor, for example, you can type into a computer a first draft—or just a portion of a first draft—and store that material on a computer disk. Later, you can retrieve the material and revise it. Word processing makes it easy to insert words into, or delete words from, your text and to shift a word or a block of words from one part of the text to another. Moreover, you can then produce a printed version of the revision without having to retype the whole corrected draft, as you would with a typewriter.

You begin your work with a word processor by creating a file and giving that file a name. If you are drafting a document, such as your thesis statement, outline, or the paper itself, it is best to create a different file for each draft. For example, assign your first drafts such labels as "thesis1," "outline1," "paper1," and store each file when finished. When you are ready to revise the draft, create a new file for the second draft ("thesis2," "outline2," "paper2"), merge the first-draft file with the new file, and revise. In this way, if you become dissatisfied with the way a second or subsequent draft is progressing, you can erase the draft, return to the preceding draft, which is stored untouched on the disk, and begin the revision all over again.

Word processors similarly allow for more efficient transitions between writing stages. If you have developed your outline, for instance, and are ready to begin writing your paper, you may transfer the outline file to a text file and use the outline as the basis for the text itself.

Another advantage to using a word processor in preparing a research paper is that you can compile your bibliography at your convenience. You need not wait until you have completed your paper or even your research but can prepare the bibliography in stages as you do your research. Whenever you wish to begin—probably when you have your research well under way and know several works you intend to use in the paper—create a file with a self-explanatory label, such as "bibliog." Then type in the works in alphabetical order, setting down each in correct form and including all the bibliographical information needed for the list of works cited (see 1.4 and ch. 4), and store the file when finished. If you later want to add new works to the list, delete works you no longer think helpful, or correct entries already stored, you retrieve the file, make the changes, and store the revised file for future use. At any stage you can also produce a printed version of the file for review. When you have finished the final draft of the text of your paper and are ready to add the list of works cited, you transfer the completed bibliography file to the end of the file containing the paper.

A word processor can also be used to store and retrieve notes, a use that might not necessarily save time but should improve the accuracy with which you transcribe material, including quotations, from your sources into the text of your paper. One way to proceed is to create a new file for each source, enter your notes for the work, and store the file. When subsequently drafting the paper, you can, at the appropriate place in the text, merge the file for the source with the file you are using for the paper, retain what you want from the source (e.g., a useful quotation), delete the rest, and proceed with the draft. At an intermediate stage between taking notes and writing the paper, you may want to create a file for each major topic of your outline and to shift relevant material, in appropriate order, from source files into the various topic files. Then, as you write, you can call up the topic files one by one and incorporate material from them into the text of the paper.

A simpler strategy for using the word processsor during note-taking is to enter into computer files only quotations you think you may use and to retrieve these, as needed, when writing. At the very least, this strategy will eliminate the time and effort and, more important, the possibility of error involved in transcribing quoted words more than once. Instead of transcribing a quotation from the source into your notes and from your notes into the text of your paper, as you would if using a typewriter, you copy it only once into a computer file and retrieve that file as needed.

In working on a computer file, of course, you run the risk of losing it, through either a technical mistake or a power failure. Be sure, then, not only to store a file when you are finished with it or when you leave the computer but also periodically (after every page or so) to "save" the material you have entered. It might also be a good idea in the later stages of the project to create a "backup disk"—that is, to copy all the files onto a second computer disk—just in case something happens to the disk you are using to prepare the paper.

Not all word-processing programs can produce the various specifications for a research paper contained in this handbook. Some, for example, measure space in inches and not in characters. If you are using such a program and cannot, say, indent each paragraph "five spaces," use the closest approximation your program can produce.

1.10. Language and style

Effective writing depends as much on clarity and readability as on content. The organization and development of your ideas, the unity and coherence of your presentation, and your command of sentence structure, grammar, and diction are all important considerations, as are the mechanics of writing—capitalization, spelling, punctuation, and so on. The key to successful communication is using the right language. In all writing, the challenge is to find the words, phrases, clauses, sentences, and paragraphs that express your thoughts and ideas precisely and that make them interesting to others.

There is still another aspect of language to consider. In recent years, writers, teachers, and publishers have become increasingly concerned about its social connotations. The careful writer avoids statements that reflect or imply unsubstantiated generalizations about a person's age, economic class, national origin, sexual orientation, political or religious beliefs, race, or sex. Your language, in other words, should not suggest bias or prejudice toward any group. Discussions and statements concerning nondiscriminatory language have focused particular attention on avoiding language that could be labeled sexist. For example, conscientious writers no longer use *he* to refer to someone of unspecified sex—a doctor or an executive, say—lest readers infer that the statement can apply only to a man. To avoid this use of *he*, they recast sentences into the plural, specify the sex of an individual under discussion, and occasionally, if all else fails, use *he or she* or *her or him*. Careful writers also avoid designating sex with suffixes like *-man* and *-ess* and substitute nonsexist terms (police officer, flight attendant, poet, author). For advice on current practices, consult your instructor or one of the guides to nonsexist language listed below.

1.11. Guides to writing

A good dictionary is an essential tool in writing. Your instructor can recommend a standard American dictionary such as the *The American College Dictionary*, *The American Heritage Dictionary of the English Language*, *The Random House Dictionary of the English Language*, or *Webster's New Collegiate Dictionary*. Because dictionaries vary in matters such as hyphenation and the preferred spelling of words, you should, to maintain consistency, use the same one throughout your paper.

You should also keep on hand at least one reliable guide to writing. Your instructor can help you choose among the many available. A selected list of writing guides appears below, classified under four headings: handbooks of composition, dictionaries of usage, guides to nonsexist language, and books on style.

Handbooks of composition

Baker, Sheridan. *The Complete Stylist and Handbook.* 3rd ed. New York: Harper, 1984.

———. *The Practical Stylist.* 6th ed. New York: Harper, 1985.

Bell, James K., and Adrian A. Cohn. *A Handbook of Grammar, Style, and Usage.* 3rd ed. New York: Macmillan, 1981.

Corbett, Edward P. J. *The Little English Handbook: Choices and Conventions.* 5th ed. Glenview: Scott, 1987.

Crews, Frederick. *The Random House Handbook.* 4th ed. New York: Random, 1984.

Ebbitt, Wilma R., and David R. Ebbitt. *Writer's Guide and Index to English.* 7th ed. Glenview: Scott, 1982.

Elsbree, Langdon, and Gerald P. Mulderig. *The Heath Handbook of Composition.* 11th ed. Lexington: Heath, 1986.

Fear, David E., and Gerald J. Schiffhorst. *Short English Handbook.* 3rd ed. Glenview: Scott, 1986.

Fowler, H. Ramsey. *The Little, Brown Handbook.* 3rd ed. Boston: Little, 1986.

Gorrell, Robert M., and Charlton Laird. *Modern English Handbook.* 6th ed. Englewood Cliffs: Prentice, 1976.

Guth, Hans P. *Words and Ideas: A Handbook for College Writing.* 5th ed. Belmont: Wadsworth, 1980.

Heffernan, James A. W., and John E. Lincoln. *Writing: A College Handbook.* 2nd ed. New York: Norton, 1986.

Hodges, John C., and Mary E. Whitten. *Harbrace College Handbook.* 10th ed. New York: Harcourt, 1986.

Irmscher, William F. *The Holt Guide to English: A Contemporary Handbook of Rhetoric, Language, and Literature.* 3rd ed. New York: Holt, 1981.

Leggett, Glenn C., David Mead, and Melinda G. Kramer. *Prentice-Hall Handbook for Writers.* 9th ed. Englewood Cliffs: Prentice, 1985.

McCrimmon, James M., Joseph F. Trimmer, and Nancy I. Sommers. *Writing with a Purpose.* 8th ed. Boston: Houghton, 1984.

McPherson, Elizabeth, and Gregory Cowan. *Plain English Please: A Rhetoric.* 5th ed. New York: Random, 1986.

Troyka, Lynn Quitman. *Simon and Schuster Handbook for Writers.* Englewood Cliffs: Prentice, 1987.

Watkins, Floyd C., and William B. Dillingham. *Practical English Handbook.* 7th ed. Boston: Houghton, 1986.

Dictionaries of usage

Bernstein, Theodore. *The Careful Writer: A Modern Guide to English Usage.* New York: Atheneum, 1965.

Bryant, Margaret M. *Current American Usage: How Americans Say It and Write It.* New York: Funk, 1962.

Copperud, Roy H. *American Usage and Style: The Consensus.* New York: Van Nostrand, 1980.

Evans, Bergen, and Cornelia Evans. *Dictionary of Contemporary American Usage.* New York: Random, 1957.

Follett, Wilson. *Modern American Usage: A Guide.* Ed. Jacques Barzun. New York: Hill, 1966.

Fowler, H[enry] W. *A Dictionary of Modern English Usage.* Ed. Ernest Gowers. 2nd ed. New York: Oxford UP, 1965.

Mager, Nathan H., and Sylvia K. Mager. *Encyclopedic Dictionary of English Usage.* Englewood Cliffs: Prentice, 1974.

Morris, William, and Mary Morris. *Harper Dictionary of Contemporary Usage.* 2nd ed. New York: Harper, 1985.

Nicholson, Margaret. *A Dictionary of American-English Usage Based on Fowler's* Modern English Usage. New York: Oxford UP, 1957.

Weiner, E. S. C. , and J. M. Hawkins. *The Oxford Guide to the English Language.* New York: Oxford UP, 1984.

Guides to nonsexist language

Cofer, Charles N., Robert S. Daniels, Frances Y. Dunham, and Walter Heimer. "Guidelines for Nonsexist Language in APA Journals." *American Psychologist* 32 (1977): 486–94.

Miller, Casey, and Kate Swift. *The Handbook of Nonsexist Writing.* New York: Lippincott, 1980.

Pickens, J. E., P. W. Rao, and L. C. Roberts, eds. *Without Bias: A Guidebook for Nondiscriminatory Communication.* San Francisco: Intl. Assn. of Business Communicators, 1977.

Books on style

Barzun, Jacques. *Simple and Direct: A Rhetoric for Writers.* Rev. ed. New York: Harper, 1984.

Beardsley, Monroe C. *Thinking Straight: Principles of Reasoning for Readers and Writers*. 4th ed. Englewood Cliffs: Prentice, 1975.

Cook, Claire Kehrwald. *Line by Line: How to Edit Your Own Writing.* Boston: Houghton, 1985.

Eastman, Richard M. *Style: Writing and Reading as the Discovery of Outlook.* 3rd ed. New York: Oxford UP, 1984.

Elbow, Peter. *Writing with Power: Techniques for Mastering the Writing Process*. New York: Oxford UP, 1981.

———. *Writing without Teachers*. New York: Oxford UP, 1973.

Gibson, Walker. *Tough, Sweet, and Stuffy: An Essay on Modern American Prose Styles*. Bloomington: Indiana UP, 1966.

Gowers, Ernest. *The Complete Plain Words*. Ed. Bruce Fraser. 2nd ed. Baltimore: Penguin, 1975.

Lanham, Richard A. *Style: An Anti-Textbook.* New Haven: Yale UP, 1974.

Smith, Charles K. *Styles and Structures: Alternative Approaches to College Writing.* New York: Norton, 1974.

Strunk, William, Jr., and E. B. White. *The Elements of Style*. 3rd ed. New York: Macmillan, 1979.

White, Edward M. *The Writer's Control of Tone*. New York: Norton, 1970.

Williams, Joseph M. *Style: Ten Lessons in Clarity and Grace.* 2nd ed. Glenview: Scott, 1985.

2. THE MECHANICS OF WRITING

Although the scope of this book precludes a detailed discussion of grammar, usage, style, and related aspects of writing, this chapter addresses questions that commonly arise about mechanical considerations in research papers:

1. Spelling
2. Punctuation
3. Names of persons
4. Numbers
5. Titles in the research paper
6. Quotations
7. Capitalization and personal names in languages other than English

2.1. Spelling

2.1.1. Consistency

Spelling, including hyphenation, should be consistent throughout the research paper—except in quotations, which must retain the spelling of the original. To ensure accuracy and consistency, always adopt the spelling that your dictionary gives first in an entry.

2.1.2. Word division

Avoid dividing words at the end of a line. If the word you are about to type will not fit on the line, you may leave the line short and begin the word on the next line. Word-processing programs with "automatic wordwrap" eliminate this problem: if a word is too long to fit on a line, the program automatically moves it to begin the next line. If you choose to divide a word, consult your dictionary about where the break should occur.

2.1.3. Foreign words

If you are quoting from a foreign language, reproduce all accents and other marks exactly as they appear in the original (école, frère, tête, leçon, Fähre, año). If these marks are not available on your typewriter or word processor, write them in by hand.

2.2. Punctuation

2.2.1. Consistency

The primary purpose of punctuation is to ensure the clarity and readability of your writing. Although punctuation is, to some extent, a matter of personal preference, there are many required uses, and while certain practices are optional, consistency is mandatory. Be sure to use the same punctuation in parallel situations.

2.2.2. Apostrophes

Apostrophes indicate contractions (rarely acceptable in research papers) and possessives. To form the possessive of a singular noun, add an apostrophe and an *s* (the accountant's ledger, television's influence); to form the possessive of a plural noun ending in *s*, add only an apostrophe (the accountants' ledgers, the soldiers' weapons). Some irregular plurals require an apostrophe and an *s* (the media's role, women's studies). All singular proper nouns, including the names of persons and places, form their possessives in the same manner (Mars's wrath, Camus's novel, Kansas's weather, Dickens's popularity, Jones's batting average, *but* the Dickenses' economic problems, the Joneses' estate).

Also use apostrophes to form the plurals of letters (*p*'s and *q*'s; *A*'s, *B*'s, *C*'s), but do not use them in the plurals of abbreviations or numbers (PhDs, MAs, VCRs, IRAs, 1990s, fours, SATs in the 700s).

2.2.3. Colons

A colon indicates that what follows will be an example, explanation, or elaboration of what has just been said. Do not use a colon where a semicolon is appropriate (see 2.2.12).

In this sentence, what follows the colon explains what precedes the colon:

```
She was sympathetic to both sides of the issue:
tradition encouraged her to vote for the bill,
but experience urged her to vote against it.
```

But this sentence contains two independent ideas and thus uses a semicolon:

```
She was sympathetic to both sides of the issue;
time now demanded that she choose one side over
the other.
```

Colons commonly introduce quotations (see 2.6.2–3, 2.6.6) and, with few exceptions, separate titles from subtitles (*Strategic Defense Initiative: The Bottom Line*).

In references and bibliographic citations, colons separate volume numbers from page numbers (3: 81–112), the city of publication from the name of the book publisher (New York: Norton, 1988), and the date of publication from the page numbers of an article in a periodical (15 Feb. 1986: 10–15). Skip only one space after a colon, never two.

2.2.4. Commas

Commas are required in the following instances:

between items in a series

```
The experience demanded blood, sweat, and tears.
```

between coordinate adjectives

We listened to an absorbing, frightening account of the event.

before coordinating conjunctions joining independent clauses

Congress passed the bill by a wide margin, and the president signed it into law.

around parenthetical elements

The invention, the first in a series during that decade, completely changed people's lives.

after fairly long phrases or clauses preceding the main clauses of sentences

After carefully studying all the available historical documents and personal writings, scholars could come to no definitive conclusion.

Commas are also used in dates (June 23, 1988; *but* 23 June 1988), before abbreviations after names (Cal Ripken, Jr., and Walter J. Ong, SJ; *but* John Hayes III), and in addresses (Rosemary Brady of 160 Carroll Street, Brooklyn, New York, visited her sister in Brooklyn, Maryland). Never use a comma and a dash or an opening parenthesis together. If the context requires a comma after a parenthetical remark (as it does here), the comma follows the closing parenthesis. (See 2.6.6 for commas with quotations; consult the index for the uses of the comma in documentation and bibliography.)

2.2.5. Dashes

To indicate a dash in typing, use two hyphens, with no space before, between, or after. Do not overuse dashes, substituting them for other punctuation marks. The dash may be used in the following instances:

around parenthetical elements that represent a break in the flow of thought

```
The low unemployment figures--New York City, for
example, had its lowest rate in twenty years--
masked the growing social unrest.
```

around parenthetical elements that require a number of internal commas

```
Many twentieth-century American writers--
Faulkner, Capote, Styron, Welty, to name only a
few--come from the South.
```

before a summarizing appositive

```
Computer chips, integrated circuits, bits, and
bytes--these new terms baffled yet intrigued.
```

2.2.6. Exclamation points

Except in direct quotation, do not use exclamation points in research writing.

2.2.7. Hyphens

Hyphens connect numbers indicating a range (1–20) and also form some types of compound words, particularly compound words that precede the words they modify (a well-established policy, a first-rate study). Hyphens also join prefixes to capitalized words (pre-Renaissance, post-Renaissance, *but* prepuberty, postnasal drip) and link pairs of coequal nouns (singer-songwriter, scholar-athlete). Many other word combinations, however, are written as one word (hardworking employees, storytelling) or as two or more words (social security tax, ad hoc committee). Note especially that adverbs ending in *ly* do not form hyphenated compounds (a wildly successful debut). Consult a standard dictionary or writing manual for guidance on the hyphenation of specific terms.

2.2.8. Italics

Italic is a type style with characters that slant upward to the right (*Casablanca*). Words that would be italicized in print should be underlined (and not printed in a slanted style) on your typewriter or computer printer. Some titles are italicized, as are letters, words, or phrases cited as linguistic examples, words referred to as words, and foreign words in an English text. The numerous exceptions to this last rule include quotations entirely in another language; non-English titles of short works (poems, short stories, essays, articles), which are placed in quotation marks and not underlined; proper names; and foreign words anglicized through frequent use. Since American English rapidly naturalizes words, use a dictionary to decide whether a foreign expression requires italics. Adopted foreign words, abbreviations, and phrases commonly not underlined include cliché, détente, e.g., et al., etc., genre, hubris, laissez-faire, raison d'être, roman à clef, tête-à-tête, and versus.

Italics for emphasis (Booth *does* contend, however . . .) is a device that rapidly becomes ineffective. It is rarely appropriate in research writing.

2.2.9. Parentheses

Parentheses (opening parenthesis to the left, closing parenthesis to the right) enclose parenthetical remarks that break too sharply with the surrounding text to be enclosed in commas. Parentheses sometimes dictate a greater separation than dashes would, but often either set of marks is acceptable, the choice depending on the other punctuation required in the context. Parentheses are used around documentation within the text (see 5.2), around explanatory comments following quotations (see 2.6.5), and around publication information in notes (see 5.8.3).

2.2.10. Periods

Periods end declarative sentences, notes, and complete blocks of information in bibliographic citations. Periods between numbers indicate related parts of a work (1.2 for act 1, scene 2; 9.3–4 for book 9, lines 3 and 4).

The period follows a parenthesis that falls at the end of a sentence. It goes within the parenthesis when the enclosed element is independent (see not this sentence but the next). (For the use of periods with ellipsis points, see 2.6.4.)

2.2.11. Quotation marks

Quotation marks should enclose quoted material (see 2.6), certain titles (see 2.5.3), and words or phrases purposely misused or used in a special sense (their "friend" brought about their downfall).

Use double quotation marks around parenthetical translations of words or phrases from another language, but use single quotation marks for definitions or translations that appear without intervening punctuation (*ainsi* 'thus'). Single quotation marks also enclose quotations within quotations (see 2.6.6) and some titles within titles (see 2.5.4).

2.2.12. Semicolons

Semicolons are used in the following instances:

between items in series when some of the items require internal commas

In one day the indefatigable candidate campaigned in Vail, Colorado; Columbus, Ohio; Nashville, Tennessee; and Teaneck, New Jersey.

between closely related independent clauses not joined by coordinating conjunctions

```
On the one hand, demand is steadily decreasing;
on the other, production keeps inexplicably
increasing.
```

before coordinating conjunctions linking independent clauses that require a number of internal commas

```
The overture begins with a brooding, mournful
passage in the strings and woodwinds, one of the
composer's most passionate statements; but the
piece concludes with a burst of lively,
spirited, almost comic music in the brass and
percussion.
```

For the use of semicolons in bibliographies and parenthetical documentation, see 4.5.20 and 5.5.8–9.

2.2.13. Slashes

Slashes (or virgules) separate lines of poetry incorporated into the text (see 2.6.3), elements in dates expressed exclusively in digits (2/12/84), and, occasionally, alternative words (and/or). Use a space before and after the slash only when separating lines of poetry.

2.2.14. Square brackets

Use square brackets around a parenthesis within a parenthesis (to avoid two pairs of parentheses), around an interpolation in a quotation (see 2.6.5), and around missing or unverified data in documentation (see 4.5.25). Insert square brackets by hand if they are not available on your typewriter or word processor.

2.3. Names of persons

2.3.1. First and subsequent uses of names

In general, the first time you use a person's name in the text of your research paper, state it fully and accurately, exactly as it appears in your source.

```
Arthur George Rust, Jr.
Victoria M. Sackville-West
```

Do not change *Arthur George Rust, Jr.* to *Arthur George Rust* or drop the hyphen in *Victoria M. Sackville-West.* In subsequent uses of the name, you may give the person's last name only (Sackville-West)—unless, of course, you refer to two or more persons with the same last name—or give the most common form of the person's name (Michelangelo for Michelangelo Buonarroti; Surrey for Henry Howard, earl of Surrey; Disraeli for Benjamin Disraeli, first earl of Beaconsfield). In some languages (e.g., Chinese, Hungarian, Japanese, Korean, and Vietnamese), surnames precede given names; consult reference works for guidance with these names. For rules concerning names of persons in other languages, see 2.7.

2.3.2. Titles of persons

In general, do not use formal titles (Mr., Mrs., Miss, Ms., Dr., Professor, Reverend) in referring to men or women, living or dead (Churchill, *not* Mr. Churchill; Einstein, *not* Professor Einstein; Hess, *not* Dame Hess; Montagu, *not* Lady Montagu). A few women in history are traditionally known by their titles as married women (e.g., Mrs. Humphry Ward, Mme de Staël). Otherwise, treat women's names the same as men's.

First use

Emily Dickinson
Harriet Beecher Stowe
Margaret Mead

Thereafter

Dickinson (not Miss Dickinson)
Stowe (not Mrs. Stowe)
Mead (not Ms. Mead)

2.3.3. Names of authors and fictional characters

It is common and acceptable to use simplified names of famous authors (Vergil for Publius Vergilius Maro, Dante for Dante Alighieri). Treat pseudonyms like ordinary names.

Molière (Jean-Baptiste Poquelin)
Voltaire (François-Marie Arouet)
George Sand (Amandine-Aurore-Lucie Dupin)
George Eliot (Mary Ann Evans)
Mark Twain (Samuel Clemens)
Stendhal (Marie-Henri Beyle)
Novalis (Friedrich von Hardenberg)

Refer to fictional characters in the same way that the work of fiction does. You need not always use their full names, and you may retain titles (Mme Defarge, Dr. Jekyll).

2.4. Numbers

2.4.1. Arabic numerals

Although there are still a few well-established uses for roman numerals (see 2.4.7), the common practice today is to represent virtually all numbers by arabic numerals. If your typewriter does not have the number *1*, use a small letter el (*l*), not capital *I*, for the arabic numeral.

2.4.2. Use of words or numerals

In general, write as words all whole numbers from one to nine and use numerals for all numbers 10 and over (about 500 years ago). But never begin a sentence with a numeral (Five hundred years ago . . .). Always use numerals with abbreviations or symbols (6 lbs., 8KB, 4 p.m., $9, 3%, 2") and in addresses (5 13th Avenue), dates (1 April 1984), decimal fractions (8.3), and page references (page 7). For very large numbers you may use a combination of numerals and words (4.5 million). Express related numbers in the same style (5 out of 217 British troops, 3 automobiles and 12 trucks, from 1 billion to 1.2 billion).

In discussions involving infrequent use of numbers, you may spell out numbers that can be written in no more than two words and represent other numbers by numerals (one, thirty-six, ninety-nine, one hundred, fifteen hundred, two thousand, three million; *but* 2½, 101, 137, and 1,275).

2.4.3. Commas in numbers

Commas are usually placed between the third and fourth digits from the right, the sixth and seventh, and so on.

```
1,000  20,000  7,654,321
```

Exceptions to this practice include page and line numbers, addresses, and four-digit year numbers. Commas are added in longer year numbers.

```
On page 3322. . . .

At 4132 Broadway. . . .

In 1999. . . .
```

but

```
In 20,000 BC. . . .
```

2.4.4. Percentages and amounts of money

Treat percentages and amounts of money like other numbers: use numerals with the appropriate symbols (1%, 45%, 100%, $5.35, $35,

$2,000, 68¢). In discussions involving infrequent use of numbers, you may spell out percentages and amounts of money if you can do so in no more than two or three words (five dollars, forty-five percent, two thousand dollars, sixty-eight cents). Do not combine spelled forms of numbers with symbols.

2.4.5. Dates

Be consistent in writing dates: use either 22 July 1989 or July 22, 1989, but not both. (If you begin with the month, be sure to add a comma after the day and also after the year, unless another punctuation mark goes there, such as a period or a question mark.) Do not use a comma between month and year (August 1987).

Spell out centuries in lowercase letters (the twentieth century) and hyphenate them as adjectives (eighteenth-century thought, nineteenth- and twentieth-century literature). Decades are usually written out without capitalization (the eighties), but it is becoming acceptable to express them in figures (the 1980s or the '80s). Whichever form you use, be consistent.

BC follows the year, but *AD* precedes it (19 BC, AD 565; some writers use *BCE*, before the Common Era, and *CE*, Common Era).

2.4.6. Inclusive numbers

In indicating a range of numbers, give the second number in full for numbers through 99 (2–3, 10–12, 21–48, 89–99). For larger numbers, give only the last two digits of the second number, unless more are necessary (96–101, 103–04, 395–401, 923–1003, 1003–05, 1608–774). In giving a range of years, write both in full unless they are within the same century (1898–1901, 1898–99).

2.4.7. Roman numerals

Use capital roman numerals for the primary divisions of an outline and for individuals in a series (Henry VIII, John Paul II, Elizabeth II). Use lowercase roman numerals for citing pages of a book that are so numbered (e.g., the pages in a preface). Your instructor may also prefer that you use roman numerals to designate acts and scenes of plays.

2.5. Titles of works in the research paper

2.5.1. Capitalization and punctuation

Always take the title of a work from the title page, not from the cover or from the top of each page. Do not reproduce any unusual typographical characteristics, such as all capital letters or the uncommon use of lowercase letters: MODERNISM & NEGRITUDE should appear as *Modernism and Negritude*; **BERNARD BERENSON** The Making of a Connoisseur as *Bernard Berenson: The Making of a Connoisseur*; Turner's early sketchbooks as *Turner's Early Sketchbooks*.

The rules for capitalizing titles are strict. In both titles and subtitles, capitalize the first words, the last words, and all principal words, including those that follow hyphens in compound terms. Therefore, capitalize nouns, pronouns, verbs, adjectives, adverbs, and subordinating conjunctions (although, if, because), but not articles (a, an, the), prepositions (e.g., in, to, of, between), coordinating conjunctions (e.g., and, or, but, nor, for), or the *to* in infinitives, when such words fall in the middle of the title. Unless the title itself has ending punctuation, use a colon and a space to separate a title from a subtitle. Include other punctuation only if it is part of the title.

Death of a Salesman

The Teaching of Spanish in English-Speaking Countries

Storytelling and Mythmaking: Images from Film and Literature

Life As I Find It

What Is Literature?

Whose Music? A Sociology of Musical Language

Where Did You Go? Out. What Did You Do? Nothing.

"Ode to a Nightingale"

"Italian Literature before Dante"

"What Americans Stand For: Two Views"

"Why Fortinbras?"

When a line of a poem or of a prose work serves as the title or part of the title, however, reproduce the line exactly as it appears in print.

"I heard a Fly buzz--when I died--"

For rules concerning capitalization of titles in languages other than English, see 2.7.

2.5.2. Underlined titles

In general, underline the titles of works published independently (for the titles of works published within larger works, see 2.5.3). Titles to be underlined include the names of books, plays, long poems published as books, pamphlets, periodicals (newspapers, magazines, and journals), films, radio and television programs, record albums, ballets, operas, instrumental musical compositions (except those identified simply by form, number, and key), paintings, works of sculpture, ships, aircraft, and spacecraft. In the following examples note that the underlining is not broken between words. While there is no need to underline the spaces between words, a continuous line is easier to type, and it guards against the error of failing to underline the punctuation within a title.

The Awakening (book)

Romeo and Juliet (play)

The Waste Land (long poem published as a book)

New Jersey Driver Manual (pamphlet)

Wall Street Journal (newspaper)

Time (magazine)

It's a Wonderful Life (film)

Star Trek (television program)

Sgt. Pepper's Lonely Hearts Club Band (record album)

The Nutcracker (ballet)

Rigoletto (opera)

Berlioz's Symphonie fantastique (instrumental musical composition identified by name)

Beethoven's Symphony no. 7 in A (instrumental musical composition identified by form, number, and key)

Chagall's I and My Village (painting)

French's The Minute Man (sculpture)

HMS Vanguard (ship)

Spirit of St. Louis (aircraft)

2.5.3. Titles in quotation marks

Use quotation marks for the titles of works published within larger works (the article "Crime Rate Declines" appeared in the *San Francisco Chronicle*). Such titles include the names of articles, essays, short stories, short poems, chapters of books, and individual episodes of radio and television programs—all works that appear within larger works. Also use quotation marks for songs and for unpublished works, such as lectures and speeches.

"Rise in Aid to Children Is Proposed" (newspaper article)

"Sources of Energy in the Twenty-First Century" (magazine article)

"Etruscan" (encyclopedia article)

"The Fiction of Langston Hughes" (essay in a book)

"The Lottery" (short story)

"Kubla Khan" (poem)

"Mood Indigo" (song)

"The American Economy before the Civil War" (chapter in a book)

"The Trouble with Tribbles" (episode of the television program *Star Trek*)

"Preparing for a Successful Interview" (lecture)

2.5.4. Titles within titles

If a title indicated by quotation marks (e.g., a short story) appears within an underlined title (e.g., a book of short stories), retain the quotation marks.

<u>"The Lottery" and Other Stories</u> (book)

If a title indicated by underlining (e.g., a play) appears within a title enclosed by quotation marks (e.g., an article about the play), retain the underlining.

"<u>Romeo and Juliet</u> and Renaissance Politics" (article)

When a title normally indicated by quotation marks (e.g., a poem) appears within another title requiring quotation marks (e.g., an article about the poem), enclose the shorter (interior) title in single quotation marks.

"An Interpretation of Coleridge's 'Kubla Khan'" (article)

When a normally underlined title (e.g., a novel) appears within another underlined title (e.g., a book about the novel), neither underline the shorter (interior) title nor put it in quotation marks.

<u>Approaches to Teaching Chopin's</u> The Awakening (book)

2.5.5. Exceptions

The convention of using underlining or quotation marks to indicate titles does not apply to sacred writings (including all books and versions of the Bible); names of series, editions, societies, buildings, and monuments; descriptive words or phrases used instead of actual titles; and names of conferences, seminars, workshops, and courses. These all appear without underlining or quotation marks.

Sacred writings

Bible	Gospels
King James Version	Talmud
Old Testament	Koran
Genesis	Upanishads

Series

Bollingen Series
University of North Carolina Studies in Comparative Literature
Masterpiece Theatre

Editions

New Variorum Edition of Shakespeare
Centenary Edition of the Works of Nathaniel Hawthorne

Societies

American Medical Association
Renaissance Society of America

Buildings and monuments

Moscone Center

Sears Tower

Arch of Constantine

Descriptive words or phrases

Roosevelt's first inaugural address

Lincoln's Gettysburg address

Conferences, seminars, workshops, and courses

Strengthening the Cooperative Effort in Biomedical Research: A National Conference for Universities and Industry

Geographic Information Analysis Workshop

MLA Annual Convention

Introduction to Calculus

Anthropology 102

Words designating the divisions of a work are also not underlined or put within quotation marks, nor are they capitalized when used in the text.

preface	chapter 2
introduction	act 4
bibliography	scene 7
appendix	stanza 20
index	canto 32

2.5.6. Shortened titles

If you cite a title often in the text of your paper, you may, after stating the title in full at least once, use only a shortened title (preferably a familiar or obvious one) or an abbreviation ("Nightingale" for "Ode to a Nightingale"; FCC for Federal Communications Commission; for standard abbreviations of literary and religious works, see 6.7).

2.6. Quotations

2.6.1. Use of quotations

While quotations are common and often effective in research papers, use them selectively. Quote only words, phrases, lines, and passages that are particularly interesting, vivid, unusual, or apt, and keep all quotations as brief as possible. Overquotation can bore your readers and might lead them to conclude that you are neither an original thinker nor a skillful writer.

In general, a quotation—whether a word, phrase, sentence, or more—should correspond exactly to its source in spelling, capitalization, and interior punctuation. If you change it in any way, make the alteration clear to the reader, following the rules and recommendations explained below.

2.6.2. Prose

If a prose quotation runs no more than four typed lines and requires no special emphasis, put it in quotation marks and incorporate it in the text.

```
"It was the best of times, it was the worst of
times," wrote Charles Dickens of the eighteenth
century.
```

Remember, though, that you need not always reproduce complete sentences. Sometimes you may want to quote just a word or phrase as part of your sentence.

For Charles Dickens the eighteenth century was both "the best of times" and "the worst of times."

You may put a quotation at the beginning, middle, or end of your sentence or, for the sake of variety or better style, divide it by your own words.

Joseph Conrad writes of the company manager in <u>Heart of Darkness</u>, "He was obeyed, yet he inspired neither love nor fear, nor even respect."

or

"He was obeyed," writes Conrad of the company manager in <u>Heart of Darkness</u>, "yet he inspired neither love nor fear, nor even respect."

If a quotation ending a sentence requires a parenthetical reference, place the sentence period after the reference. (For more information on punctuating quotations, see 2.6.6.)

For Charles Dickens the eighteenth century was both "the best of times" and "the worst of times" (35).

"He was obeyed," writes Conrad of the company manager in <u>Heart of Darkness</u>, "yet he inspired neither love nor fear, nor even respect" (87).

If a quotation runs to more than four typed lines, set it off from your text by beginning a new line, indenting ten spaces from the left margin, and typing it double-spaced, without adding quotation marks. A colon generally introduces a quotation displayed in this way, though sometimes the context may require a different mark of punctuation, or none at all. If you are quoting only a single paragraph, or part of one, do not indent the first line more than the rest. When adding a parenthetical reference to a prose quotation set off from the text, skip two spaces after the quotation and give the reference.

At the conclusion of Lord of the Flies Ralph and the other boys realize the horror of their actions:

> The tears began to flow and sobs shook him. He gave himself up to them now for the first time on the island; great, shuddering spasms of grief that seemed to wrench his whole body. His voice rose under the black smoke before the burning wreckage of the island; and infected by that emotion, the other little boys began to shake and sob too. And in the middle of them, with filthy body, matted hair, and unwiped nose, Ralph wept for the end of innocence. . . . (186)

In quoting two or more paragraphs, indent the first line of each paragraph an additional three spaces. If, however, the first sentence quoted does not begin a paragraph in the source, do not indent it the additional three spaces. Indent only the first lines of the successive paragraphs.

2.6.3. Poetry

If you quote a single line of verse, or part of a line, that does not require special emphasis, put it in quotation marks within your text. You may also incorporate two or three lines in this way, using a slash with a space on each side (/) to separate them. (In the following examples, note that verse plays are cited by division and line rather than by page numbers; *Julius Caesar* 5.5.74, for instance, refers to act 5, scene 5, line 74 of the play [see 5.5.8].)

In Shakespeare's Julius Caesar, Antony says of Brutus: "This was the noblest Roman of them all" (5.5.74).

"Friends, Romans, countrymen," begins Antony's famous speech, "lend me your ears; / I come to bury Caesar, not to praise him" (3.2.80-81).

Verse quotations of more than three lines should begin on a new line. Unless the quotation involves unusual spacing, indent each line ten spaces from the left margin and double-space between lines, adding no quotation marks that do not appear in the original. Brief parenthetical references for verse quotations set off from the text appear two spaces after the quotation (as in quotations of prose); parenthetical references that will not fit comfortably on the same line as the last line of the quotation should begin a new line.

Elizabeth Bishop's "In the Waiting Room" is rich in evocative detail:

> It was winter. It got dark
> early. The waiting room
> was full of grown-up people,
> arctics and overcoats,
> lamps and magazines. (6-10)

If the lines quoted are so long that a ten-space indentation would make the page look unbalanced, you may indent fewer than ten spaces from the margin. And if the spatial arrangement of the original, including indentation and spacing within and between lines, is unusual, reproduce it as accurately as possible.

E. E. Cummings concludes the poem with this vivid description of a carefree scene, reinforced by the carefree form of the lines themselves:

```
          it's
          spring
          and
              the
                 goat-footed
          balloonMan     whistles
          far
          and
          wee  (16-24)
```

A quotation that begins in the middle of the line of verse should be reproduced in that way and not shifted to the left margin.

Jaques in <u>As You Like It</u> is given the speech that many think contains a glimpse of Shakespeare's conception of drama:

```
                              All the world's a stage
          And all the men and women merely players:
          They have their exits and their entrances;
          And one man in his time plays many parts,
          His acts being seven ages.  (2.7.147-51)
```

Jaques then proceeds to enumerate and analyze these ages.

2.6.4. Ellipsis

When you wish to omit a word, phrase, sentence, or paragraph from a quoted passage, you should be guided by two principles: (1) fairness to the author quoted and (2) the grammatical integrity of your own writing. If you quote only a word or a phrase, it will be obvious that you have left out some of the original sentence.

In his inaugural address, John F. Kennedy spoke of a "new frontier."

But if omitting material from the original leaves a quotation that appears to be a sentence, or a series of sentences, you must use ellipsis points, or spaced periods, to indicate that your quotation does not completely reproduce the original.

For an ellipsis *within* a sentence, use three periods with a space before and after each one (. . .).

Original

Medical thinking, trapped in the theory of astral influences, stressed air as the communicator of disease, ignoring sanitation or visible carriers. (From Barbara W. Tuchman, *A Distant Mirror: The Calamitous Fourteenth Century*, 1978; New York: Ballantine, 1979, 101–02.)

Quoted with an ellipsis in the middle

In seeking causes for plagues in the Middle Ages, as Barbara W. Tuchman writes, "Medical thinking . . . stressed air as the communicator of disease, ignoring sanitation or visible carriers."

Quoted with an ellipsis in the middle, with a parenthetical reference

In seeking causes for plagues in the Middle Ages, as Barbara W. Tuchman writes, "Medical

thinking . . . stressed air as the communicator of disease, ignoring sanitation or visible carriers" (101-02).

When the ellipsis coincides with the end of your sentence, use three spaced periods following a sentence period—that is, four periods, with no space before the first.

Quoted with an ellipsis at the end

In seeking causes for plagues in the Middle Ages, as Barbara W. Tuchman writes, "Medical thinking, trapped in the theory of astral influences, stressed air as the communicator of disease. . . ."

If a parenthetical reference follows the ellipsis at the end of your sentence, use three spaced periods and place the sentence period after the final parenthesis.

Quoted with an ellipsis at the end, followed by a parenthetical reference

In seeking causes for plagues in the Middle Ages, as Barbara W. Tuchman writes, "Medical thinking, trapped in the theory of astral influences, stressed air as the communicator of disease . . ." (101-02).

Four periods can also indicate the omission of a whole sentence or more, or even of a paragraph or more. Remember, however, that grammatically complete sentences must both precede and follow the four periods.

Original

Presidential control reached its zenith under Andrew Jackson, the extent of whose attention to the press even before he became a candidate is suggested by the fact that he subscribed to twenty newspapers. Jackson was never content to have only one organ grinding out his tune. For a time, the *United States Telegraph* and the *Washington Globe* were almost equally favored as party organs, and there were fifty-seven journalists on the government payroll.
(From William L. Rivers, *The Mass Media: Reporting, Writing, Editing*, 2nd ed., New York: Harper, 1975, 7.)

Quoted with the omission of a complete sentence

In discussing the historical relation between politics and the press, William L. Rivers notes, "Presidential control reached its zenith under Andrew Jackson. . . . For a time, the <u>United States Telegraph</u> and the <u>Washington Globe</u> were almost equally favored as party organs, and there were fifty-seven journalists on the government payroll" (7).

The omission of words and phrases from quotations of poetry that are set off from the text is indicated by three or four spaced periods (as in quotations of prose). The omission of a line or more, however, is indicated by a line of spaced periods approximately the length of a complete line of the quoted poem.

Original

In Worcester, Massachusetts,
I went with Aunt Consuelo
to keep her dentist's appointment
and sat and waited for her
in the dentist's waiting room.
It was winter. It got dark
early. The waiting room
was full of grown-up people,
arctics and overcoats,
lamps and magazines.
(From Elizabeth Bishop, "In the Waiting Room," lines 1–10)

Quoted with an omission of a line or more in the middle

Elizabeth Bishop's "In the Waiting Room" is rich in evocative detail:

In Worcester, Massachusetts,
I went with Aunt Consuelo
to keep her dentist's appointment
. . . .
It was winter. It got dark
early. (1-3, 6-7)

Quoted with an ellipsis at the end

Elizabeth Bishop's "In the Waiting Room" is rich in evocative detail:

In Worcester, Massachusetts,
I went with Aunt Consuelo
to keep her dentist's appointment
and sat and waited for her
in the dentist's waiting room.
It was winter. It got dark
early. The waiting room
was full of grown-up people. . . . (1-8)

2.6.5. Other alterations of sources

Occasionally, you may decide that a quotation will be unclear or confusing to your reader unless you provide supplementary information. While you may add material to a quoted source, just as you may omit it, you should keep such contributions to a minimum and make sure to distinguish them from the original, usually by putting them in square brackets within the quotation or by explaining them in parentheses after the quotation.

A comment or explanation that goes inside the quotation must appear within square brackets, not parentheses. (If your typewriter does not include square brackets, insert them by hand.)

The title of the student's paper was "My Interpretation of 'Imitations of Immorality' [sic]."

Similarly, if a pronoun seems unclear in a quotation, you may add an identification in square brackets.

    Why, she would hang on him [Hamlet's father]
As if increase of appetite had grown
By what it fed on. . . .

An explanation in parentheses—for example, an indication that you have underlined words for emphasis immediately follows the closing quotation mark.

Lincoln specifically advocated a government "for the people" (emphasis added).

Without the parenthetical addition, readers would assume that the word underlined in the quotation is italicized in the original. Or you may need to add *sic* (Latin for "thus" or "so") in parentheses to assure readers that the quotation is accurate even though the spelling or logic might lead them to think otherwise.

The student referred to "Imitations of Immorality" (sic) as one of Wordsworth's famous poems.

The accuracy of quotations in research writing is extremely important. They must reproduce the original exactly. Unless indicated in brackets or parentheses, liberties must not be taken with the spelling or the punctuation of the source. In short, you must construct a clear, grammatically correct sentence that allows you to introduce or incorporate a quotation with complete accuracy. Alternatively, you can paraphrase the original and quote only fragments, which may be easier to integrate into the text. Methods vary, as the following examples show.

Original

Moralists have unanimously agreed, that unless virtue be nursed by liberty, it will never attain due strength—and what they say of man I extend to mankind, insisting that in all cases morals be fixed on immutable principles; and, that the being cannot be termed rational or virtuous, who obeys any authority, but that of reason. (From Mary Wollstonecraft, *A Vindication of the Rights of Woman*, ed. Carol H. Poston, New York: Norton, 1975, 191.)

If you wish to begin your sentence with *unless*, the sixth word of the Wollstonecraft passage, you must capitalize the *u* and place it in brackets to indicate your alteration of the source. But if you would rather not use square brackets to begin the sentence, you can recast the sentence.

Mary Wollstonecraft wrote that "unless virtue be nursed by liberty, it will never attain due strength . . ." (191).

2.6.6. Punctuation with quotations

As the proceeding sections explain, you often need slashes, parentheses, and brackets to present quotations accurately. Also commonly required are preceding commas or colons. Use a colon before a quotation you formally introduce but either no punctuation or a comma before a quotation you integrate into the sentence.

Shelley argued thus: "Poets are the unacknowledged legislators of the World" (794).

but

Shelley thought poets "the unacknowledged legislators of the World" (794).

or

"Poets," according to Shelley, "are the unacknowledged legislators of the World" (794).

A colon normally precedes a verse quotation, as it does any quotation set off from the text.

Coleridge's <u>Rime of the Ancient Mariner</u> concludes: "A sadder and a wiser man, / He rose the morrow morn" (624-25).

Do not use opening and closing quotation marks to enclose quotations set off from the text, but generally reproduce internal punctuation exactly as in the original. Use double quotation marks for quotations incorporated into the text, single quotation marks for quotations within those quotations.

In "Kitchenette Building," Gwendolyn Brooks writes: "'Dream' makes a giddy sound, not strong / Like 'rent,' 'feeding a wife,' 'satisfying a man'" (2-3).

Although the internal punctuation of a quotation must remain intact, the closing punctuation depends on where the quoted material appears in your sentence. Suppose, for example, that you want to quote the following sentence.

You've got to be carefully taught.

If you begin your sentence with this line, you have to replace the closing period with a punctuation mark appropriate to the new context.

"You've got to be carefully taught," wrote Oscar Hammerstein II of racial prejudice.

If the quotation ends with a question mark or an exclamation point, however, the original punctuation is retained and no comma is required.

"How can I describe my emotions at this catastrophe, or how delineate the wretch whom with such infinite pains and care I had endeavoured to form?" wonders the doctor in Mary Shelley's Frankenstein (42).

"What a wonderful little almanac you are, Celia!" Dorothea Brooke responds to her sister (7).

By convention, commas and periods that directly follow quotations go inside the closing quotation marks, but a parenthetical reference should intervene between the quotation and the required punctuation. Thus, if the quotation ends with a period, the period appears after the reference.

N. Scott Momaday's House Made of Dawn begins with an image that also concludes the novel: "Abel was running" (7).

If a quotation ends with both single and double quotation marks, the comma or period precedes both:

"Read 'Kubla Khan,'" he told me.

All other punctuation marks—such as semicolons, colons, question marks, and exclamation points—go outside quotation marks, except when they are part of the quoted material.

Original

I believe taxation without representation is tyranny!

Quoted

He attacked "taxation without representation" (32).

Did he attack "taxation without representation"?

He did not even attack "taxation without representation"!

but

He declared that "taxation without representation is tyranny!"

If a quotation ending with a question mark or an exclamation point concludes your sentence and requires a parenthetical reference, retain the original punctuation within the quotation marks and follow with the reference and the sentence period outside the quotation marks.

In Mary Shelley's Frankenstein, the doctor wonders, "How can I describe my emotions at this catastrophe, or how delineate the wretch whom with such infinite pains and care I had endeavoured to form?" (42).

Dorothea Brooke responds to her sister, "What a wonderful little almanac you are, Celia!" (7).

2.7. Capitalization and personal names in languages other than English

The following section contains rules for writing personal names and for capitalizing in French, German, Italian, Spanish, and Latin. If you need such rules for other languages or if you need information on transliteration from languages using different alphabets, such as Russian or Chinese, consult *The MLA Style Manual*.

2.7.1. French

Personal names

With some exceptions, French *de* following a first name or a title such as *Mme* or *duc* is not used with the last name alone:

La Boétie, Etienne de
La Bruyère, Jean de
Maupassant, Guy de
Nemours, duc de
Ronsard, Pierre de
Scudéry, Madeleine de

When the last name has only one syllable, however, *de* is usually retained:

de Gaulle, Charles

The preposition also remains, in the form *d'*, when it elides with a last name beginning with a vowel:

d'Arcy, Pierre
d'Arsonval, Arsène

Similarly the forms *du* and *des*—combinations of *de* with a following *le* or *les*—are always used with the last name:

Des Périers, Bonaventure
Du Bartas, Guillaume de Salluste

A hyphen is normally used between French given names (M.-J. Chénier is Marie-Joseph Chénier, but M. R. Char is Monsieur René Char, and P. J. Reynard is Père J. Reynard).

Capitalization

In prose or verse, French usage is the same as English except that the following terms are not capitalized unless they begin sentences or, sometimes, lines of verse: (1) the subject pronoun *je* 'I,' (2) days and months, (3) the names of languages and the adjectives derived from proper nouns, (4) titles preceding personal names and the words for street, square, and similar places.

```
Un Français m'a parlé anglais près de la place
de la Concorde.

Hier j'ai vu le docteur Maurois qui conduisait
une voiture Ford.

Le capitaine Boutillier m'a dit qu'il partait
pour Rouen le premier jeudi d'avril avec
quelques amis normands.
```

In both titles and subtitles, capitalize the first words and all proper nouns.

<u>Du côté de chez Swann</u>

<u>Le grand Meaulnes</u>

<u>La guerre de Troie n'aura pas lieu</u>

<u>Nouvelle revue des deux mondes</u>

<u>L'ami du peuple</u>

Some instructors, however, follow other rules. When the title of a work begins with an article, they also capitalize the first noun and any preceding adjectives. In titles of series and periodicals, they capitalize all major words.

2.7.2. German

Personal names

German *von* is generally not used with the last name alone, but there are some exceptions, especially in English contexts, where the *von* is firmly established by convention.

Droste-Hülshoff, Annette von
Kleist, Heinrich von

but

Von Braun, Wernher
Von Trapp, Maria

Alphabetize German names with umlauts (ä, ö, ü) without regard to the umlaut. Do not substitute a two-letter combination for a vowel with an umlaut; for example, do not convert *ü* to *ue*.

Capitalization

In prose or verse, German usage is the same as English, with some important exceptions. Always capitalized in German are (1) all substantives, including any adjectives, infinitives, pronouns, prepositions, or other parts of speech used as substantives, and (2) the pronoun *Sie* 'you' and its possessive *Ihr* 'your' and their inflected forms. Not capitalized unless they begin sentences or, usually, lines of verse are (1) the subject pronoun *ich* 'I,' (2) days of the week or names of languages used as adjectives, adverbs, or complements of prepositions, and (3) adjectives and adverbs formed from proper nouns, except that those derived from personal names are always capitalized when they refer explicitly to the works and deeds of those persons.

Ich glaube an das Gute in der Welt.

Er schreibt, nur um dem Auf und Ab der Buch-
Nachfrage zu entsprechen.

Fahren Sie mit Ihrer Frau zurück?

Ein französischer Schriftsteller, den ich gut
kenne, arbeitet sonntags immer an seinem neuen
Buch über die platonische Liebe.

Der Staat ist eine der bekanntesten Platonischen
Schriften.

In letters and ceremonial writings, the pronouns *du* and *ihr* 'you' and their derivatives are capitalized.

In titles and subtitles, capitalize the first words and all words normally capitalized.

Ein treuer Diener seines Herrn
Thomas Mann und die Grenzen des Ich
Zeitschrift für vergleichende Sprachforschung

2.7.3. Italian

Personal names

The names of many Italians who lived before or during the Renaissance are alphabetized by first name.

Bonvesin da la Riva
Cino da Pistoia
Dante Alighieri

Iacopone da Todi
Michelangelo Buonarroti

But other names of the period follow the standard practice.

Boccaccio, Giovanni
Cellini, Benvenuto
Stampa, Gaspara

The names of members of historic families are also usually alphabetized by last name.

Este, Beatrice d'
Medici, Lorenzo de'

In modern times, the Italian *da*, *de*, *del*, *della*, and *di* are used with the last name. They are usually capitalized and are treated as an integral part of the name, even though a space may separate the prepositional from the nominal part of the name.

D'Annunzio, Gabriele
De Sanctis, Francesco
Del Buono, Oreste
Della Casa, Giovanni
Di Costanzo, Angelo

Capitalization

In prose or verse, Italian usage is the same as English except that centuries and other large divisions of time are capitalized and the following terms are not capitalized unless they begin sentences or, usually, lines of verse: (1) the subject pronoun *io* 'I,' (2) days and months, (3) names of languages, (4) nouns, adjectives, and adverbs derived from proper nouns, and (5) titles preceding personal names and the words for street, square, and similar places.

Un italiano parlava francese con uno svizzero in piazza di Spagna.

```
Il dottor Bruno ritornerà dall'Italia giovedì
otto agosto e io partirò il nove.
```

```
la lirica del Novecento
il Rinascimento
```

In both titles and subtitles, capitalize only the first words and all words normally capitalized.

<u>Dizionario letterario Bompiani</u>
<u>Bibliografia della critica pirandelliana</u>
<u>L'arte tipografica in Urbino</u>
<u>Collezione di classici italiani</u>
<u>Studi petrarcheschi</u>

2.7.4. Spanish

Personal names

Spanish *de* is not used before the last name alone.

Las Casas, Bartolomé de
Madariaga, Salvador de
Rueda, Lope de
Timoneda, Juan de

Spanish *del*, formed from the fusion of the preposition *de* and the definite article *el*, must be used with the last name: Del Río, Angel.

Spanish surnames often include both the paternal name and the maternal name, with or without the conjunction *y*. The surname of a married woman usually includes her paternal surname and her husband's paternal surname, connected by *de*. Alphabetize Spanish names by the full surnames (consult your sources or a biographical dictionary for guidance in distinguishing surnames and given names).

Álvarez, Miguel de los Santos
Cervantes Saavedra, Miguel de
Díaz del Castillo, Bernal
Figuera Aymerich, Ángela
Larra y Sánchez de Castro, Mariano José
López de Ayala, Pero
Matute, Ana María
Ortega y Gasset, José
Quevedo y Villegas, Francisco Gómez de
Sinues de Marco, María del Pilar
Zayas y Sotomayor, María de

Even persons commonly known by the maternal portions of their surnames, such as Galdós and Lorca, should be indexed under their full surnames:

García Lorca, Federico
Pérez Galdós, Benito

Capitalization

In prose or verse, Spanish usage is the same as English except that the following terms are not capitalized unless they begin sentences or, sometimes, lines of verse: (1) the subject pronoun *yo* 'I,' (2) days and months, (3) nouns or adjectives derived from proper nouns, (4) titles preceding personal names and the words for streets, squares, and similar places.

```
El francés hablaba inglés en la plaza Colón.

Ayer yo vi al doctor García en un coche Ford.

Me dijo don Jorge que iba a salir para Sevilla
el primer martes de abril con unos amigos
neoyorkinos.
```

In both titles and subtitles, capitalize only the first words and words normally capitalized.

Historia verdadera de la conquista de la Nueva España

La gloria do don Ramiro

Extremos de América

Trasmundo de Goya

Breve historia del ensayo hispanoamericano

Revista de filología española

2.7.5. Latin

Personal names

Roman male citizens generally had three names: a praenomen (given name), a nomen (clan name), and a cognomen (family or familiar name). Men in this category are usually referred to by nomen, cognomen, or both; your source or a standard reference book such as the *Oxford Classical Dictionary* will provide guidance.

Brutus (Marcus Iunius Brutus)
Calpurnius Siculus (Titus Calpurnius Siculus)
Cicero (Marcus Tullius Cicero)
Lucretius (Titus Lucretius Carus)
Plautus (Titus Maccius Plautus)

Roman women usually had two names: a nomen (the clan name in the feminine form) and a cognomen (often derived from the father's cognomen): Livia Drusilla (daughter of Marcus Livius Drusus). Sometimes a woman's cognomen indicates her chronological order among the daughters of the family: Antonia Minor (younger daughter of Marcus Antonius). Most Roman women are referred to by nomen: Calpurnia, Clodia, Octavia, Sulpicia. Some, however, are better known by cognomen: Agrippina (Vipsania Agrippina).

When citing Roman names, use the forms most common in English:

Horace (Quintus Horatius Flaccus)
Julius Caesar (Gaius Iulius Caesar)
Juvenal (Decimus Iunius Iuvenalis)
Livy (Titus Livius)
Ovid (Publius Ovidius Naso)
Quintilian (Marcus Fabius Quintilianus)
Terence (Publius Terentius Afer)
Vergil (Publius Vergilius Maro)

Finally, some medieval and Renaissance figures are best known by their adopted or assigned Latin names:

Albertus Magnus (Albert von Bollstädt)
Comenius (Jan Amos Komenský)
Copernicus (Niklas Koppernigk)
Paracelsus (Theophrastus Bombast von Hohenheim)

Capitalization

Although practice varies, Latin most commonly follows the English rules for capitalization, except that *ego* 'I' is not capitalized.

Semper ego auditor tantum? Numquamne reponam / Vexatus totiens rauci Theseide Cordi?

Quidquid id est, timeo Danaos et dona ferentes.

Nil desperandum.

Quo usque tandem abutere, Catilina, patientia nostra?

In both titles and subtitles, however, capitalize only the first words and all words normally capitalized.

<u>De senectute</u>

<u>Liber de senectute</u>

<u>Medievalia et humanistica</u>

3. THE FORMAT OF THE RESEARCH PAPER

If your instructor has specific requirements for the format of a research paper, check these before preparing your final draft. The following recommendations are the most common.

3.1. Typing or printing

Use clean type and either a carbon ribbon or a fresh black cloth ribbon. Avoid typewriters or printers with "script" or other fancy print. A letter-quality printer is preferable to a dot-matrix printer; when using a printer, do not justify the lines of your paper. Type or print on only one side of the paper; do not use the other side for any purpose. Instructors who accept handwritten work also require neatness, legibility, dark blue or black ink, and the use of only one side of the paper. Be sure to keep a copy of the paper.

3.2. Paper

Use only white, twenty-pound, 8½- by 11-inch paper. Do not submit work typed on erasable paper, which smudges easily. If you find erasable paper convenient to use for your final draft, submit a photocopy to your instructor.

3.3. Margins

Except for page numbers, leave one-inch margins at the top and bottom and on both sides of the text. (For placement of page numbers, see 3.6.) Indent the first word of a paragraph five spaces from the left margin. Indent set-off quotations ten spaces from the left margin. (For examples, see section 2.6 and the sample first page of a research paper at the end of this book.)

3.4. Spacing

The research paper must be double-spaced throughout, including quotations, notes, and the list of works cited. If you are using a word processor, begin the file by setting the document for double spacing. In a handwritten paper, indicate double spacing by skipping one ruled line. (See the sample pages of a research paper at the end of this book.)

3.5. Heading and title

A research paper does not need a title page. Instead, beginning one inch from the top of the first page and flush with the left margin, type your name, your instructor's name, the course number, and the date on separate lines, double-spacing between the lines. Double-space again and center the title. Double-space also between the lines of the title, and double-space between the title and the first line of the text.

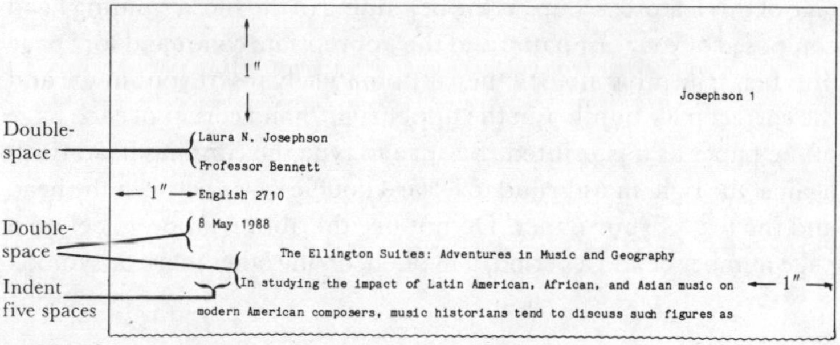

Do not underline your title or put it in quotation marks or type it in all capital letters. Follow the rules for capitalization in 2.5.1, and underline only those words that you would underline in the text (see 2.2.8).

Local Television Coverage of Recent

International News Events

The Attitude toward Violence in Anthony

Burgess's <u>A Clockwork Orange</u>

Vergil and the Locus Amoenus Tradition in Latin
  Literature
The Use of the Noun Chevisaunce in Chaucer and
  Spenser

Do not use a period after your title or after any heading (e.g., Works Cited).

3.6. Page numbers

Number all pages consecutively throughout the manuscript in the upper right-hand corner, one-half inch from the top. Type your last name before the page number, as a precaution in case of misplaced pages. Word processors with automatic page numbering will save you the time and effort of having to number every page. To take advantage of this feature, set up, at the beginning of the file, a running head composed of your last name and the appropriate command for "page number"; the program will then automatically insert your name and the correct page number in the upper right-hand corner of each page of the paper as it is printed. Be sure to type the running head flush against the right margin and to leave a double space between the head and the text of your paper. Do not use the abbreviation *p.* before a page number or add a period, a hyphen, or any other mark or symbol.

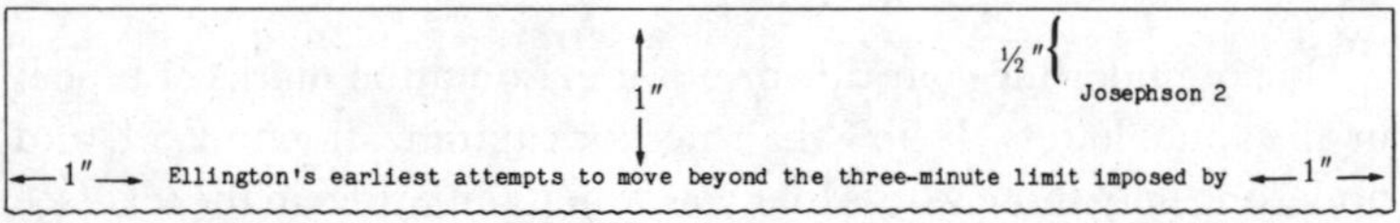

3.7. Tables and illustrations

Place illustrative material as close as possible to the part of the text that it illustrates. A table is usually labeled "Table," given an arabic numeral, and captioned. Type both label and caption flush left on

Table 1

Language Immersion Program of the State University of New York, New Paltz

Weekend Immersion Program Enrollment[a]

Language	1984-85	1985-86
American Sign	6	4
Arabic	29	12
Chinese	19	11
French	429	408
German	123	145
Greek	12	--
Hebrew	18	5
Italian	170	160
Japanese	55	46
Polish	14	8
Portuguese	9	1
Russian	52	79
Spanish	328	345
Swedish	10	19
Yiddish	22	15
Total	1,296	1,258

Source: Henry Urbanski, "The Language Immersion Program at New Paltz," <u>ADFL Bulletin</u> 18.3 (1987): 58.

[a] Weekend courses are offered in New Paltz and New York City.

separate lines above the table and capitalize them as you would a title (do not use all capital letters). Give the source of the table and any notes immediately below the table. To avoid any confusion between notes to the text and notes to the table, designate notes to the table with lowercase letters rather than numerals. Double-space throughout, making ruled lines as needed.

Any other type of illustrative material—for example, a photograph, map, line drawing, graph, or chart—should be labeled "Figure" (usually abbreviated "Fig."), assigned an arabic numeral, and given a title or caption (Fig. 1. Mary Cassatt, *Mother and Child*, Wichita Art Museum, Wichita). A label, title, or caption is ordinarily given directly below the illustration, flush with the left margin.

Fig. 1. Unicorn, woodcut from Edward Toppsell, The History of Four-Footed Beasts and Serpents . . . (London, 1658) 551; rpt. in Konrad Gesner, Curious Woodcuts of Fanciful and Real Beasts (New York: Dover, 1971) 27.

3.8. Corrections and insertions

Proofread and correct your research paper carefully before submitting it. If your instructor permits brief corrections, type them (or write them neatly and legibly in ink) directly above the lines involved, using carets (^) to indicate where they go. Do not use the margins or write below a line. If corrections on any one page are numerous or substantial, retype the page. If you are using a word processor, recall the file, make the appropriate revisions, and reprint the page or pages.

3.9. Binding

Although a plastic folder or some other kind of binder may seem an attractive finishing touch to your research paper, most instructors find such devices a nuisance in reading and commenting on students' work. Staples and pins are similarly annoying, since they are bothersome to take out and replace. Of course, pages may get misplaced or lost if they are left unattached or merely folded down at the upper left-hand corners. Secure the pages of your paper with a paper clip, which can be easily removed and restored.

4. PREPARING THE LIST OF WORKS CITED

4.1. General guidelines

In writing a research paper, you must indicate exactly where you found whatever material you borrow—whether facts, opinions, or quotations. This handbook recommends that you acknowledge your sources by keying citations in the text to a list of the research materials you have used. Although this list will appear at the end of your paper, you should draft it in advance, recording the works you plan to mention so that you will know what information to give in parenthetical references as you write. This chapter explains how to prepare a list of works cited, and the next chapter demonstrates how to document sources where you use them in your text. (For information on other systems of documentation, such as endnotes and footnotes, see 5.7–8.)

The **Works Cited** section of your paper should list all the works that you have cited in your text. It simplifies documentation because it permits you to make only brief references to these works in the text. A citation such as "(Thompson 32–35)" enables readers to identify the source in the Works Cited. Other names for such a listing are **Bibliography** (literally, "description of books") and **Literature Cited**. Usually, however, the broader title **Works Cited** is more appropriate, since research papers often draw on not only books and articles but also films, recordings, television programs, and other nonprint sources.

Titles used for other kinds of source lists include **Annotated Bibliography**, **Works Consulted**, and **Selected Bibliography**. An **Annotated Bibliography**, or an **Annotated List of Works Cited**, contains descriptive or evaluative comments on the sources.

```
Thompson, Stith.  The Folktale.  New York:
     Dryden, 1946.  A comprehensive survey of
     the most popular folktales, including their
     histories and their uses in literary works.
```

The title **Works Consulted** indicates that the list is not confined to works cited in the paper. A **Selected Bibliography**, or a **Selected List of Works Consulted**, suggests readings in the field.

4.2. Placement

The list of works cited appears at the end of the paper. Begin the list on a new page and number each page, continuing the page numbers of the text. For example, if the text of your research paper ends on page 10, the Works Cited will begin on page 11. Type the page number in the upper right-hand corner, one-half inch from the top, and center the title Works Cited one inch from the top of the page. Double-space between the title and the first entry. Begin each entry flush with the left margin, and if it runs more than one line, indent the subsequent line or lines five spaces from the left margin. Double-space the entire list, both between and within entries. Continue the list on as many pages as necessary.

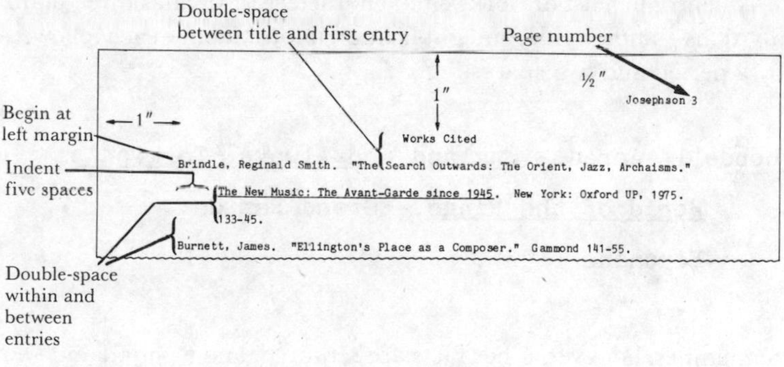

4.3. Arrangement

In general, alphabetize entries in the list of works cited by the author's last name, using the letter-by-letter system: *MacDonald, George* comes before *McCullers, Carson*; *Saint-Saens, Camille* before *St. Denis, Ruth.* For alphabetizing foreign names, see 2.7. If the author's name is unknown, alphabetize by the first word in the title other than *A*, *An*, or *The* (*An Encyclopedia of the Latin-American Novel* would be alphabetized under *E*). The alphabetical listing, as explained at greater length in the next chapter, makes it easy for the reader to find full publication information for works referred to in the text.

Other kinds of bibliographies may be arranged differently. An annotated list, a list of works consulted, or a list of selected readings for a historical study, for example, may be organized chronologically by publication date. Some bibliographies are divided into sections, with the items alphabetized in each. A list may be broken down into primary sources and secondary sources or into different research media (books, articles, recordings). Alternatively, it may be arranged by subject matter (Literature and Law, Law in Literature, Law as Literature), by period (Classical Utopia, Renaissance Utopia), or by area (Egyptian Mythology, Greek Mythology, Norse Mythology).

4.4. Citing books: Information required

4.4.1. General guidelines

An entry in a list of works cited characteristically has three main divisions—author, title, and publication information—each followed by a period and two spaces.

Lobdell, Jared. England and Always: Tolkien's World of the Rings. Grand Rapids: Eerdmans, 1981.

Sometimes, however, other facts are required, and a period and two spaces follow each additional item of information.

Porter, Katherine Anne. "Flowering Judas." Norton Anthology of World Masterpieces. Ed. Maynard Mack et al. 5th ed. Vol. 2. New York: Norton, 1986. 1698-1709. 2 vols.

In citing books, normally arrange the information in the following order:

1. Author's name
2. Title of a part of the book
3. Title of the book
4. Name of the editor, translator, or compiler
5. Edition used
6. Number(s) of the volume(s) used
7. Name of the series
8. Place of publication, name of the publisher, and date of publication
9. Page numbers
10. Supplementary bibliographic information and annotation

Sections 4.4.2–11 give general recommendations for citing these items of information, and section 4.5 provides examples.

4.4.2. Author's name

Reverse the author's name for alphabetizing, adding a comma after the last name (Porter, Katherine Anne). Put a period after the name and leave two spaces before beginning the next item. (On citing books by two or more persons, see 4.5.4.)

Apart from reversing the order, give the author's name as it appears on the title page. Never abbreviate a name given in full. If, for example, the title page lists the author as *Carleton Brown*, do not enter the book under *Brown, C.* But use initials if the title page does.

Eliot, T. S.

McLuhan, H. Marshall.

You may use square brackets to indicate a full name not found in the work cited if you think this additional information would be helpful to readers. You might supply it, for example, if you use the full name in your text or if another source uses it.

Hinton, S[usan] E[loise].

Tolkien, J[ohn] R[onald] R[euel].

Similarly, use square brackets if you wish to indicate the real name of an author listed under a pseudonym.

```
Le Carré, John [David Cornwell].
Svevo, Italo [Ettore Schmitz].
```

In general, omit titles, affiliations, and degrees that precede or follow names. For example, Anthony T. Boyle, PhD; Sister Jean Daniel; Reverend Theodore M. Hesburgh; Gerard Manley Hopkins, SJ; Lady Mary Wortley Montagu; Sir Philip Sidney; Dame Joan Sutherland; and Saint Teresa de Jesús would appear in your list of works cited as follows:

```
Boyle, Anthony T.
Daniel, Jean.
Hesburgh, Theodore M.
Hopkins, Gerard Manley.
Montagu, Mary Wortley.
Sidney, Philip.
Sutherland, Joan.
Teresa de Jesús.
```

Suffixes that are an essential part of the name—like *Jr.* or a roman numeral—appear after the given name.

```
Rockefeller, John D., IV.
Rust, Arthur George, Jr.
```

Occasionally, it is more appropriate to begin an entry by naming not the author but the editor or translator (see 4.5.2, 4.5.12–13). To cite an anonymous book or a book by a corporate author, see 4.5.6–7; a work written by more than one author, 4.5.4; two or more books by the same author or authors, 4.5.3–4.

4.4.3. Title of a part of the book

In general, follow the recommendations for titles given in 2.5. To cite only a part of a book, state the title or name of the part of the book after the author's name. Place a period after the title of a part of a book, skip two spaces, and begin the next item. To cite a work in an anthology (e.g., an essay, a short story, a poem, or a play), see 4.5.8; for a book division that has only a general name (e.g., an introduction or a preface), see 4.5.9; for two or more pieces from a single book, see 4.5.10.

4.4.4. Title of the book

In general, follow the recommendations for titles given in 2.5. State the full title of the book, including any subtitle. If a book has a subtitle, put a colon directly after the title, unless the title itself ends in a punctuation mark (e.g., a question mark, an exclamation point, or a period), and skip a space before giving the subtitle. Place a period after the entire title (including any subtitle), unless it ends in another punctuation mark, and skip two spaces before beginning the next item. Type a line under the entire title, including the colon, the subtitle, and whatever punctuation the title contains, but do not underline the period that follows the title.

When an *or* precedes the subtitle, capitalize the conjunction and the next word, separating the two by a comma.

```
"Criticulture: Or, Why We Need at Least Three
     Criticisms at the Present Time."
```

4.4.5. Name of the editor, translator, or compiler

If the name of an editor, translator, or compiler appears on the title page, it is usually appropriate to include this information after the title of the work, preceded by the appropriate abbreviation (Ed., Trans., Comp.). If someone has served in more than one role—say, as editor and translator—state those roles in the order in which they appear on the title page.

```
Ed. and trans. Fred J. Nichols.
```

Similarly, if different persons served in such roles, give the names in the order in which they appear on the title page.

```
Trans. Walter Arndt.  Ed. Cyrus Hamlin.
```

For examples, see especially 4.5.8, 12–13. To cite writers of introductions, prefaces, forewords, and afterwords, see 4.5.9.

4.4.6. Edition used

A book that gives no edition number or name on its title page is probably a first edition, as your reader will assume if your bibliographic entry does not indicate otherwise. If, however, you are using a later edition of a work, identify it in your entry by number (2nd ed., 3rd ed., 4th ed.), by name (Rev. ed., for "revised edition") or by year (1988 ed.)—whichever the title page indicates. Works revised on an annual or other regular basis commonly designate successive editions by year (see 4.5.15).

4.4.7. Number(s) of the volume(s) used

In citing a multivolume work, state the complete number of volumes if you use more than one volume of the work (3 vols.). But if you use only one volume of the work, state the number of that volume alone (Vol. 2). In such instances, you may include the complete number of volumes as supplementary information at the end of the listing (see 4.5.11).

4.4.8. Name of the series

In citing a book that is part of a publication series, give the name of the series and the arabic numeral denoting the work's place in the series (see 4.5.18).

4.4.9. Place of publication, name of the publisher, and date of publication

Give the city of publication, the publisher's name, and the year of publication (for a few exceptions, see 4.5.15 and 4.5.24–25). Take these facts directly from the book itself, not from a source such as a bibliography or a library catalog. Publication information usually appears on the title page, the copyright page (i.e., the reverse of the title page), or, particularly in books published outside the United States, the colophon at the back of the book. Use a colon and a space between the place of publication and the publisher, a comma and a space between the publisher and the date, and a period after the date.

Since the city of publication is sometimes needed to identify a book, it should always be given. If several cities are listed for the publisher, give only the first. For cities outside the United States, add an abbreviation of the country (or province for cities in Canada) if the name of the city may be ambiguous or unfamiliar to your reader (Manchester, Eng.; Sherbrooke, PQ; see 6.3 for abbreviations of geographical names). To cite the city of publication for a book published in a language other than English, see 4.5.22. If no place of publication is given, write *N.p.* for "no place" (see 4.5.25).

Use an appropriately shortened form of the publisher's name, following the guidelines in 6.5. To cite a work issued under a publisher's special imprint, give the imprint and add the publisher's name after a hyphen (Anchor-Doubleday; see 4.5.19). If the title page indicates that two publishers have brought out the work simultaneously, give both (see 4.5.20). You may omit the name of a publisher for a work published before 1900 (see 4.5.24). If no publisher is given for a later work, write *n.p.* for "no publisher" after the colon (see 4.5.25); if a work is privately printed, write *privately printed* (see 4.5.27).

After the publisher's name, a comma, and a space, write the year in which the book was published. If this date is not recorded on the title or copyright page or in the colophon, use the latest copyright date. If the copyright page indicates that the work has had several printings (or "impressions") by the same publisher, use the original publication date. But in citing a new or revised edition, give the date of that edition, not the original publication date. If you are listing a reprint by a different publisher—for instance, a paperback reprint of a book originally published in a clothbound edition—give the dates of both the original edition and the reprint (see 4.5.14). In citing a multivolume work published over a number of years, give the inclusive dates (see 4.5.11). If no date of publication is printed in the book, write *n.d.* (see 4.5.25) or supply in square brackets an approximate date and a question mark. If the date is known, though missing in the book, omit the question mark.

4.4.10. Page numbers

Give the inclusive page numbers when you cite part of a book (e.g., an essay, short story, or preface). Be sure to give the page numbers of the entire piece, not just the pages for the material you have used; specific page references will appear, in parentheses, within the text (see ch. 5). Inclusive page numbers, usually without any identifying abbreviation, follow the publication date, a period, and two spaces (see 4.5.8). If the book has no pagination, you may indicate *N. pag.* as part of the entry (see 4.5.25).

4.4.11. Supplementary bibliographic information and annotation

Add, if necessary or desired, supplementary bibliographic data, such as information about additional volumes of a multivolume work (see 4.5.11) or the original version of a translated work (see 4.5.13). Any other annotation or supplementary information appears at the end of the entry.

4.5. Sample entries: Books

The following examples illustrate the recommendations in 4.4.

4.5.1. A book by a single author

To cite a book by a single author, follow the general pattern outlined in 4.4: author's name (reversed for alphabetizing), title (including any subtitle), and publication information (city of publication, publisher, date of publication).

Fairbanks, Carol. Prairie Women: Images in American and Canadian Fiction. New Haven: Yale UP, 1986.

Freedman, Richard R. What Do Unions Do? New York: Basic, 1984.

Hinton, S[usan] E[loise]. Tex. New York: Delacorte, 1979.

Le Carré, John [David Cornwell]. The Little Drummer Girl. New York: Knopf, 1983.

4.5.2. An anthology or a compilation

To cite an anthology or a compilation (e.g., a bibliography), begin with the name of the editor or compiler, followed by a comma, a space, and the abbreviation *ed.* or *comp.* If the person has performed more than one function—serving, say, as editor and translator—give both roles in the order in which they appear on the title page.

Allen, Robert C., ed. Channels of Discourse: Television and Contemporary Criticism. Chapel Hill: U of North Carolina P, 1987.

Nichols, Fred J., ed. and trans. An Anthology of Neo-Latin Poetry. New Haven: Yale UP, 1979.

Sevillano, Mando, comp. The Hopi Way: Tales from a Vanishing Culture. Flagstaff: Northland, 1986.

Stratman, Carl J., comp. and ed. Bibliography of English Printed Tragedy, 1565-1900. Carbondale: Southern Illinois UP, 1966.

See also the sections on works in an anthology (4.5.8), introductions and prefaces to books (4.5.9), editions (4.5.12), and translations (4.5.13).

4.5.3. Two or more books by the same person

In citing two or more books by the same person, give the name in the first entry only. Thereafter, in place of the name, type three hyphens and a period, skip two spaces, and give the title. The three hyphens always stand for exactly the same name(s) as in the preceding entry. If the person named served as editor, translator, or compiler of any of the books, place a comma (not a period) after the three hyphens, skip a space, and write the appropriate abbreviation (ed., trans., or comp.) before giving the title. If the same person served as, say, the editor of two or more works listed consecutively, the abbreviation *ed.* must be repeated with each entry. This sort of label, however, does not affect the order in which entries appear; works listed under the same name(s) are alphabetized by title.

Borroff, Marie. Language and the Past: Verbal Artistry in Frost, Stevens, and Moore. Chicago: U of Chicago P, 1979.

---, trans. Sir Gawain and the Green Knight. New York: Norton, 1967.

---, ed. Wallace Stevens: A Collection of Critical Essays. Englewood Cliffs: Prentice, 1963.

Frye, Northrop. Anatomy of Criticism: Four Essays. Princeton: Princeton UP, 1957.

---, ed. Design for Learning: Reports Submitted to the Joint Committee of the Toronto Board of Education and the University of Toronto. Toronto: U of Toronto P, 1962.

---. The Myth of Deliverance: Reflections on Shakespeare's Problem Comedies. Toronto: U of Toronto P, 1983.

4.5.4. A book by two or more persons

In citing a book by two or three persons, give their names in the order in which they appear on the title page—not necessarily in alphabetical order. Reverse only the name of the first author, add a comma, and give the other name(s) in normal order (Wellek, René, and Austin Warren). Place a period after the last name, skip two spaces, and begin the next item. Even if the authors have the same last name, state each name in full (Durant, Will, and Ariel Durant). If the persons listed on the title page are editors, translators, or compilers, place a comma (not a period) after the final name and add the appropriate abbreviation (eds., trans., or comps.).

Berry, Jason, Jonathan Foose, and Tad Jones. Up from the Cradle of Jazz: New Orleans Music since World War II. Athens: U of Georgia P, 1986.

Gong, Victor, and Norman Rudnick, eds. AIDS: Facts and Issues. New Brunswick: Rutgers UP, 1986.

Hyde, Margaret O., and Elizabeth Held Forsyth. Suicide: The Hidden Epidemic. Rev. ed. New York: Watts, 1986.

Welsch, Roger L., and Linda K. Welsch. Cather's Kitchens: Foodways in Literature and Life. Lincoln: U of Nebraska P, 1987.

If there are more than three authors, you may name only the first and add *et al.* ("and others"), or you may give all names in full in the order in which they appear on the title page.

Edens, Walter, et al., eds. Teaching Shakespeare. Princeton: Princeton UP, 1977.

Quirk, Randolph, et al. A Comprehensive Grammar of the English Language. London: Longman, 1985.

or

Edens, Walter, Christopher Durer, Walter Eggers, Duncan Harris, and Keith Hull, eds. Teaching Shakespeare. Princeton: Princeton UP, 1977.

Quirk, Randolph, Sidney Greenbaum, Geoffrey Leech, and Jan Svartvik. A Comprehensive Grammar of the English Language. London: Longman, 1985.

If a single author cited in an entry is also the first of multiple authors in the following entry, repeat the name in full; do not substitute three hyphens. Likewise, repeat the name in full whenever you cite the same person as part of a different authorship. Remember that the three hyphens always stand for exactly the same name(s) as in the preceding entry.

Rabkin, Eric S. The Fantastic in Literature. Princeton: Princeton UP, 1976.

Rabkin, Eric S., Martin H. Greenberg, and Joseph Olander, eds. No Place Else: Explorations in Utopian and Dystopian Fiction. Carbondale: Southern Illinois UP, 1983.

Scholes, Robert. Semiotics and Interpretation. New Haven: Yale UP, 1982.

---. Textual Power: Literary Theory and the Teaching of English. New Haven: Yale UP, 1985.

Scholes, Robert, and Robert Kellogg. The Nature of Narrative. New York: Oxford UP, 1966.

Scholes, Robert, and Eric S. Rabkin. Science Fiction: History, Science, Vision. New York: Oxford UP, 1977.

4.5.5. Two or more books by the same persons

In citing two or more works by the same persons, give the names in the first entry only. Thereafter, in place of the names, type three hyphens, add a period, skip two spaces, and give the next title. The three hyphens always stand for exactly the same name(s) as in the preceding entry.

Gilbert, Sandra M. Acts of Attention: The Poems of D. H. Lawrence. Ithaca: Cornell UP, 1972.

---. Emily's Bread: Poems. New York: Norton, 1984.

Gilbert, Sandra M., and Susan Gubar. The Madwoman in the Attic: The Woman Writer and the Nineteenth-Century Literary Imagination. New Haven: Yale UP, 1979.

---, eds. The Norton Anthology of Literature by Women: The Tradition in English. New York: Norton, 1985.

4.5.6. A book by a corporate author

A corporate author may be a commission, an association, a committee, or any other group whose individual members are not identified on the title page. Cite the book by the corporate author, even if the corporate author is the publisher. (On citing government publications, see 4.5.17.)

American Library Association. *Intellectual Freedom Manual*. 2nd ed. Chicago: ALA, 1983.

American Medical Association. *The American Medical Association Family Medical Guide*. Rev. ed. New York: Random, 1987.

Commission on the Humanities. *The Humanities in American Life: Report of the Commission on the Humanities*. Berkeley: U of California P, 1980.

National Committee on Careers for Older Americans. *Older Americans: An Untapped Resource*. Washington: Acad. for Educ. Dev., 1979.

4.5.7. An anonymous book

If a book has no author's name on the title page, do not use either *Anonymous* or *Anon.* Begin the entry with the title and alphabetize by the first word other than a definite or indefinite article. (In the sample entries note that *A Guide to Our Federal Lands* is alphabetized under *G*.)

Encyclopedia of Photography. New York: Crown, 1984.

A Guide to Our Federal Lands. Washington: Natl. Geographic Soc., 1984.

<u>New Jersey: A Guide to Its Past and Present</u>.
New York: Viking, 1939.

<u>The Times Atlas of the World</u>. Rev. ed. London:
Times, 1984.

4.5.8. A work in an anthology

First, state the author and title of the piece you are citing (e.g., an essay, a short story, or a poem), normally enclosing the title in quotation marks but underlining instead if the work was originally published as a book (e.g., a play or a novel; see sample entries for Hansberry and Unamuno y Jugo). If the anthology contains works by different translators, give the translator's name next, preceded by the abbreviation *Trans.* (see entry for Unamuno y Jugo) and followed by the title of the anthology (underlined). If all the works have the same translator or if the collection has an editor, write *Trans.* or *Ed.*, or *Ed. and trans.*, after the title and give that person's name. Cite the inclusive pages for the piece at the end of the citation, after the year of publication, a period, and two spaces.

Hansberry, Lorraine. <u>A Raisin in the Sun</u>.
<u>Black Theater: A Twentieth-Century Collection of the Work of Its Best Playwrights</u>. Ed. Lindsay Patterson. New York: Dodd, 1971. 221-76.

Lazard, Naomi. "In Answer to Your Query." <u>The Norton Book of Light Verse</u>. Ed. Russell Baker. New York: Norton, 1986. 52-53.

Rubinstein, Arye. "Children with AIDS and the Public Risk." <u>AIDS: Facts and Issues</u>. Ed. Victor Gong and Norman Rudnick. New Brunswick: Rutgers UP, 1986. 99-103.

Unamuno y Jugo, Miguel de. Abel Sanchez. Trans. Anthony Kerrigan. Eleven Modern Short Novels. Ed. Leo Hamalian and Edmond L. Volpe. 2nd ed. New York: Putnam's, 1970. 253-350.

"A Witchcraft Story." The Hopi Way: Tales from a Vanishing Culture. Comp. Mando Sevillano. Flagstaff: Northland, 1986. 33-42.

In citing an article or essay in a collection of previously published works, give the complete data for the earlier publication and then add *Rpt. in* ("Reprinted in"), the title of the collection, and the new publication facts.

Holland, Norman N. "Unity, Identity, Text, Self." PMLA 90 (1975): 813-22. Rpt. in Reader-Response Criticism: From Formalism to Post-Structuralism. Ed. Jane P. Tompkins. Baltimore: Johns Hopkins UP, 1980. 118-33.

If a new title has been assigned to the piece, give the original title as well as the original publication information, followed by *Rpt. as* ("Reprinted as") and the new title and publication facts.

Lewis, C. S. "The Anthropological Approach." English and Medieval Studies Presented to J. R. R. Tolkien on the Occasion of His Seventieth Birthday. Ed. Norman Davis and C. L. Wrenn. London: Allen, 1962. 219-23.

Rpt. as "Viewpoints: C. S. Lewis." Twentieth Century Interpretations of Sir Gawain and the Green Knight. Ed. Denton Fox. Englewood Cliffs: Prentice, 1968. 100-01.

If you refer to more than one piece from the same collection, you may wish to cross-reference each citation to a single entry for the book itself (see 4.5.10). On citing introductions and prefaces, see 4.5.9. On citing a piece in a multivolume anthology, see 4.5.11.

4.5.9. An introduction, preface, foreword, or afterword

To cite an introduction, preface, foreword, or afterword, begin with the name of its author and then give the name of the part being cited, capitalized but neither underlined nor enclosed in quotation marks (Introduction, Preface, Foreword, Afterword). If the writer of the piece is different from the author of the complete work, cite the author of the work after the title, giving the full name, in normal order, preceded by the word *By*. If the writer of the piece is also the author of the complete work, use only the last name after *By*.

Borges, Jorge Luis. Foreword. Selected Poems, 1923-1967. By Borges. Ed. Norman Thomas Di Giovanni. New York: Delta-Dell, 1973. xv-xvi.

Doctorow, E. L. Introduction. Sister Carrie. By Theodore Dreiser. New York: Bantam, 1982. v-xi.

Johnson, Edgar. Afterword. David Copperfield. By Charles Dickens. New York: Signet-NAL, 1962. 871-79.

4.5.10. Cross-references

To avoid unnecessary repetition in citing two or more works from the same collection, you may list the collection itself, with complete publication information and cross-reference individual pieces to that entry. In a cross-reference, state the author and the title of the piece, the last name of the editor of the collection, and the relevant page numbers.

Atkin, Charles. "Changing Male and Female Roles." Schwarz 66-70.

Kilbourne, Jean. "Sex Roles in Advertising." Schwarz 211-15.

Schwarz, Meg, ed. TV and Teens: Experts Look at the Issues. Reading: Addison, 1982.

If you list two or more works under the editor's name, however, add the title (or a shortened version of it) to the cross-reference.

Allen, Woody. "No Kaddish for Weinstein." Howe, Jewish-American 217-21.

Howe, Irving, ed. Classics of Modern Fiction: Ten Short Novels. 2nd ed. New York: Harcourt, 1972.

---, ed. Jewish-American Stories. New York: Mentor-NAL, 1977.

James, Henry. The Pupil. Howe, Classics 189-229.

O'Connor, Flannery. The Displaced Person. Howe, Classics 469-507.

Olsen, Tillie. "Tell Me a Riddle." Howe, Jewish-American 82-117.

4.5.11. A multivolume work

If you have used two or more volumes of a multivolume work, cite the total number of volumes in the work. Add this information (5 vols.) between the title and the publication information; specific references to volume and page numbers (3: 212–13) belong in the text. (See ch. 5 for parenthetical documentation.)

If the volumes of the work were published over a period of years, give the inclusive dates at the end of the citation (1952–70). If the work is still in progress, write *to date* after the number of volumes (3 vols. to date) and leave a space after the hyphen that follows the beginning date (1982–).

Churchill, Winston S. A History of the English-Speaking Peoples. 4 vols. New York: Dodd, 1956-58.

Daiches, David. A Critical History of English Literature. 2nd ed. 2 vols. New York: Ronald, 1970.

Gracián, Baltasar. El criticón. Ed. M. Romera-Navarro. 3 vols. Philadelphia: U of Pennsylvania P, 1938-40.

Inge, M. Thomas, Maurice Duke, and Jackson R. Bryer, eds. Black American Writers: Bibliographical Essays. 2 vols. New York: St. Martin's, 1978.

Potter, G. R., et al., eds. The New Cambridge Modern History. 14 vols. Cambridge: Cambridge UP, 1957-70.

Schlesinger, Arthur M., gen. ed. History of U.S. Political Parties. 4 vols. New York: Chelsea, 1973.

Wing, Donald, et al., eds. Short-Title Catalogue of Books Printed in England, Scotland, Ireland, Wales, and British America and of English Books Printed in Other Countries, 1641-1700. 2nd ed. 3 vols. to date. New York: MLA, 1972- .

If you use only one volume of a multivolume work, include the volume number in the bibliographic entry and give the publication information for that volume; then you need give only page numbers when you refer to that work in the text. You may conclude the entry with the number of volumes for the entire work and, if the volumes were published over a period of years, the inclusive dates of publication (see sample entries for Daiches and Gracián). If the volume you use has an individual title, give that title between the author's name and the publication information for the volume. Next cite the volume number, preceded by *Vol.* and followed by the word *of*, and the title of the complete work. You may conclude the entry with the total number of volumes, and, if the work appeared over a period of years, the inclusive publication dates (see sample entry for Churchill).

Churchill, Winston S. The Age of Revolution. New York: Dodd, 1957. Vol. 3 of A History of the English-Speaking Peoples. 4 vols. 1956-58.

Daiches, David. A Critical History of English Literature. 2nd ed. Vol. 2. New York: Ronald, 1970. 2 vols.

Gracián, Baltasar. El criticón. Ed. M. Romera-Navarro. Vol. 2. Philadelphia: U of Pennsylvania P, 1939. 3 vols. 1938-40.

When citing a piece in a multivolume work, give the page number(s) after the publication information you are citing.

Mowry, George E. "The Progressive Party, 1912 and 1924." History of U.S. Political Parties. Gen. ed. Arthur M. Schlesinger. Vol. 3. New York: Chelsea, 1973. 2541-669. 4 vols.

Parry, J. H. "Latin America, 1899-1949." The New Cambridge Modern History. Vol. 12. Ed. David Thomson. Cambridge: Cambridge UP, 1964. 178-204. 14 vols. Ed. G. R. Potter et al. 1957-70.

4.5.12. An "edition"

Every published book is, in one sense, an "edition"; for example, a book may be a "first edition" or a "second edition," and so forth. Researchers also use the term *edition*, however, to denote a work by one person that has been prepared for printing by another, the editor. For example, a 1988 printing of Shakespeare's *Hamlet* was, obviously, not prepared for printing by Shakespeare. An editor selected a version of *Hamlet* from the various versions available, decided on any changes in spelling or punctuation, and perhaps added explanatory notes or wrote an introduction. This 1988 version of *Hamlet* would be called an "edition" and the name of the editor would most likely appear on the title page.

To cite an edition, begin with the author if you refer primarily to the text itself; give the editor's name, preceded by the abbreviation *Ed.*, after the title. If the book is a volume of a multivolume work edited by the same person, state the editor's name after the title of the multivolume work (see entry for Crane). If the volume editor and the general editor are not the same person, state the volume editor's name after the title of the volume and the general editor's name after the title of the multivolume work (see entry for Howells). If, for clarity's sake, you wish to indicate the original date of publication, place the year directly after the title (see entry for Crane).

Chaucer, Geoffrey. The Works of Geoffrey Chaucer. Ed. F. N. Robinson. 2nd ed. Boston: Houghton, 1957.

Crane, Stephen. The Red Badge of Courage: An Episode of the American Civil War. 1895. Charlottesville: UP of Virginia, 1975. Vol. 2 of The Works of Stephen Crane. Ed. Fredson Bowers. 10 vols. 1969-76.

Howells, W. D. Their Wedding Journey. Ed. John K. Reeves. Bloomington: Indiana UP, 1968. Vol. 5 of A Selected Edition of W. D. Howells. Gen. ed. Edwin H. Cady et al. 32 vols. 1968-83.

If you cite more than one volume of a multivolume work, give one listing for the entire work. Parenthetical references in the text will document the specific volumes you use (see ch. 5).

Dewey, John. The Early Works, 1882-1898. Ed. Jo Ann Boydston. 4 vols. Carbondale: Southern Illinois UP, 1967-71.

If your citations are generally to the work of the editor (e.g., the introduction, the notes, or editorial decisions regarding the text), begin the entry with the editor's name followed by a comma and the abbreviation *ed.*, and give the author's name, preceded by the word *By*, after the title.

Bowers, Fredson, ed. The Red Badge of Courage: An Episode of the American Civil War. By Stephen Crane. Charlottesville: UP of Virginia, 1975. Vol. 2 of The Works of Stephen Crane. 10 vols. 1969-76.

4.5.13. A translation

In citing a translation, state the author's name first if you refer primarily to the work itself; give the translator's name, preceded by *Trans.*, after the title. If the book has an editor as well as a translator, give the names, with appropriate abbreviations, in the order in which they appear on the title page (see entry for Goethe).

Calvino, Italo. The Uses of Literature. Trans. Patrick Creagh. San Diego: Harcourt, 1986.

Goethe, Johann Wolfgang von. Faust. Trans. Walter Arndt. Ed. Cyrus Hamlin. New York: Norton, 1976.

Sastre, Alfonso. Sad Are the Eyes of William Tell. Trans. Leonard Pronko. The New Wave Spanish Drama. Ed. George E. Wellwarth. New York: New York UP, 1970. 265-321.

If your citations are mostly to the translator's comments or choice of language, begin the bibliographic entry with the translator's name, followed by a comma and the abbreviation *trans.*, and give the author's name, preceded by the word *By*, after the title. (On citing anthologies of translated works by different authors, see 4.5.8.)

Arndt, Walter, trans. _Faust_. By Johann Wolfgang von Goethe. Ed. Cyrus Hamlin. New York: Norton, 1976.

Although not required, some or all of the original publication information may be added at the end of the entry.

Ducrot, Oswald, and Tzvetan Todorov. _Encyclopedic Dictionary of the Sciences of Language_. Trans. Catherine Porter. Baltimore: Johns Hopkins UP, 1979. Trans. of _Dictionnaire encyclopédique des sciences du langage_. Paris: Seuil, 1972.

Grimal, Pierre. _Love in Ancient Rome_. Trans. Arthur Train, Jr. Norman: U of Oklahoma P, 1986. Trans. of _L'amour à Rome_. 1980.

4.5.14. A republished book

In citing a republished book—for example, a paperback version of a book originally published in a clothbound version—give the original publication date, followed by a period and two spaces, before the publication information for the book you are citing. If the republished book has a new title, state the original title as well as the original publication date, followed by *Rpt. as* ("Reprinted as") and the new title and publication facts (see entry for *New Jersey*).

Douglas, Mary. _Purity and Danger: An Analysis of the Concepts of Pollution and Taboo_. 1966. London: Ark, 1984.

New Jersey: A Guide to Its Past and Present. 1939. Rpt. as The WPA Guide to 1930s New Jersey. New Brunswick: Rutgers UP, 1986.

Walker, Alice. The Color Purple. 1982. New York: Pocket, 1985.

Although not required, additional information pertaining to the original publication may precede the original publication date.

Willey, Basil. The Eighteenth Century Background: Studies on the Idea of Nature in the Thought of the Period. London: Chatto, 1940. Boston: Beacon, 1961.

If the republication adds new material, such as an introduction, include the information after the original publication facts.

Dreiser, Theodore. Sister Carrie. 1900. Introd. E. L. Doctorow. New York: Bantam, 1982.

4.5.15. An article in a reference book

Treat an encyclopedia article or a dictionary entry as you would a piece in a collection (4.5.8), but do not cite the editor of the reference work. If the article is signed, give the author first (often articles in reference books are signed with initials identified elsewhere in the work); if it is unsigned, give the title first. If the encyclopedia or dictionary arranges articles alphabetically, you may omit volume and page numbers.

When citing familiar reference books, especially those that frequently appear in new editions, do not give full publication information. For such works, list only the edition (if stated) and the year of publication.

"Azimuthal Equidistant Projection." _Webster's New Collegiate Dictionary_. 1983 ed.

Chiappini, Luciano. "Este, House of." _Encyclopaedia Britannica: Macropaedia_. 1974 ed.

"Graham, Martha." _Who's Who of American Women_. 14th ed. 1985-86.

"Melodeon." _Encyclopedia Americana_. 1985 ed.

When citing less familiar reference books, however, especially those that have appeared in only one edition, give full publication information.

Brakeley, Theresa C. "Mourning Songs." _Funk and Wagnalls Standard Dictionary of Folklore, Mythology, and Legend_. Ed. Maria Leach and Jerome Fried. 2 vols. New York: Crowell, 1950.

Trainen, Isaac N., et al. "Religious Directives in Medical Ethics." _Encyclopedia of Bioethics_. Ed. Warren T. Reich. 4 vols. New York: Free, 1978.

4.5.16. A pamphlet

Treat a pamphlet as you would a book.

Career as an Aerospace-Aircraft Engineer. Chicago: Inst. for Research, 1978.

Kilgus, Robert. _Color Scripsit Program Manual_. Fort Worth: Tandy, 1981.

4.5.17. Government publications

Because government publications emanate from many sources, they present special problems in bibliographic citation. In general, if the writer of the document is not known, cite the government agency as the author—that is, state the name of the government first, followed by the name of the agency, using an abbreviation if the context makes it clear. (But see below for citing a document whose author is known.) If you are citing two or more works issued by the same government, substitute three hyphens for the name in each entry after the first. If you also cite more than one work by the same government agency, use an additional three hyphens in place of the agency.

```
California.  Dept. of Industrial Relations.
United States.  Cong.  House.
---.  ---.  Senate.
---.  Dept. of Health and Human Services.
```

The title of the publication, underlined, should follow immediately. In citing a congressional document other than the *Congressional Record* (which requires only a date and a page number), include such information as the number and session of Congress, the house (S or HR), and the type and number of the publication. Types of congressional publications include bills (S 33, HR 77), resolutions (S. Res. 20, H. Res. 50), reports (S. Rept. 9, H. Rept. 142), and documents (S. Doc. 333, H. Doc. 222).

The usual publishing information comes next (i.e., place, publisher, and date). Most federal publications, regardless of the branch of government, are published by the Government Printing Office (GPO) in Washington, DC; its British counterpart is Her (or His) Majesty's Stationery Office (HMSO) in London. Documents issued by the United Nations and most local governments, however, do not emanate from a central office; give the publishing information that appears on the title page.

```
Cong. Rec.  7 Feb. 1973: 3831-51.
Great Britain.  Ministry of Defence.  Author and
```

Subject Catalogues of the Naval Library, Ministry of Defence. 5 vols. London: HMSO, 1967.

New York State. Committee on State Prisons. Investigation of the New York State Prisons. 1883. New York: Arno, 1974.

United Nations. Centre for National Resources. State Petroleum Enterprises in Developing Countries. Elmsford: Pergamon, 1980.

---. Economic Commission for Africa. Industrial Growth in Africa. New York: United Nations, 1963.

United States. Cong. Joint Committee on the Investigation of the Pearl Harbor Attack. Hearings. 79th Cong., 1st and 2nd sess. 32 vols. Washington: GPO, 1946.

---. ---. Senate. Subcommittee on Constitutional Amendments of the Committee on the Judiciary. Hearings on the "Equal Rights" Amendment. 91st Cong., 2nd sess. S. Res. 61. Washington: GPO, 1970.

---. Dept. of Labor. Bureau of Statistics. Dictionary of Occupational Titles. 4th ed. Washington: GPO, 1977.

---. Dept. of State. Office of Public Affairs. Korea, 1945-1947: A Report on Political Development and Economic Resources. 1948. Westport: Greenwood, 1968.

If known, the name of the document's author may either begin the entry or, if the agency comes first, follow the title and the word *By*.

Washburne, E. B. Memphis Riots and Massacres. U. S. 39th Cong., 2nd sess. H. Rept. 101. 1866. New York: Arno, 1969.

or

United States. Cong. House. Memphis Riots and Massacres. By E. B. Washburne. 39th Cong., 2nd sess. H. Rept. 101. 1866. New York: Arno, 1969.

4.5.18. A book in a series

If the title page or the preceding page (the half-title page) indicates that the book you are citing is part of a series, include the series name, neither underlined nor enclosed in quotation marks, and the series number, followed by a period, before the publishing information. Use common abbreviations for the series name, including *Ser.* if the word *series* is part of the name.

Koloski, Bernard, ed. Approaches to Teaching Chopin's The Awakening. Approaches to Teaching World Literature 16. New York: MLA, 1988.

Maravall, José Antonio. Culture of the Baroque: Analysis of a Historical Structure. Trans. Terry Cochran. Theory and History of

Literature 25. Minneapolis: U of Minnesota P, 1986.

Stewart, Joan Hinde. Colette. Twayne's World Authors Ser. 679. Boston: Twayne, 1983.

4.5.19. A publisher's imprint

Publishers often establish imprints to identify groups of books they publish. Among Doubleday's many imprints, for example, are Anchor Books, Crime Club, and Double D Western. The name of a publisher's imprint often appears above the publisher's name on the title page or on the copyright page. In citing a book published under an imprint, give the name of the imprint, followed by a hyphen and the name of the publisher (Ace-Berkeley, Camelot-Avon, Mentor-NAL).

Findlater, Jane, and Mary Findlater. Crossriggs. 1908. Introd. Paul Binding. New York: Virago-Penguin, 1986.

Kozol, Jonathan. Illiterate America. New York: Anchor-Doubleday, 1985.

4.5.20. Multiple publishers

If the title page lists two or more publishers—not just two or more offices of the same publisher—include both, in the order given, as part of the publication information, putting a semicolon after the name of the first publisher.

Duff, J. Wight. A Literary History of Rome: From the Origins to the Close of the Golden Age. Ed. A. M. Duff. 3rd ed. 1953. London: Benn; New York: Barnes, 1967.

Shelley, Percy Bysshe. Selected Poems. Ed. Timothy Webb. London: Dent; Totowa: Rowman, 1977.

4.5.21. Published proceedings of a conference

Treat the published proceedings of a conference like a book, but add pertinent information about the conference (unless the book title includes such information).

Gordon, Alan M., and Evelyn Rugg, eds. Actas del Sexto Congreso Internacional de Hispanistas celebrado en Toronto del 22 al 26 agosto de 1977. Toronto: Dept. of Spanish and Portuguese, U of Toronto, 1980.

Humanistic Scholarship in America. Proc. of a Conference on the Princeton Studies in the Humanities. 5-6 Nov. 1965. Princeton: Princeton U, 1966.

Treat a particular presentation in the proceedings like a work in a collection of pieces by different authors (see 4.5.8).

4.5.22. A book in a language other than English

Although some or all of the publication information usually found on the title or copyright page may be found in the colophon, treat a book published in a language other than English like any other book. If a clarification of the title seems necessary, provide a translation, in brackets (*Et Dukkehjem* [*A Doll House*]). Similarly, you may use brackets to give the English name of a foreign city (Wien [Vienna]); or you may substitute the English name. Use the appropriate abbreviation for the publisher's name (see 6.5). For capitalization in languages other than English, see 2.7.

Dahlhaus, Carl. Musikästhetik. Köln: Gerig, 1967.

Gramsci, Antonio. Gli intelletuali e l'organizzazione della cultura. Torino: Einaudi, 1949.

Rey-Flaud, Henri. Pour une dramaturgie du Moyen Age. Paris: PUF, 1980.

Wachowicz, Barbara. Marie jeho Života. Praha [Prague]: Lidové, 1979.

4.5.23. A book with a title within its title

If the book title you are citing contains a title normally enclosed within quotation marks (e.g., a short story or a poem), retain the quotation marks and underline the entire title. If the closing quotation mark appears at the end of the title, place a period before the quotation mark. If the title contains a title normally underlined (e.g., a novel or a play), neither underline the shorter title nor place it in quotation marks; give the shorter title in "roman type"—that is, not underlined.

Basinger, Jeanine. The It's a Wonderful Life Book. New York: Knopf, 1986.

Danzig, Allan, ed. Twentieth Century Interpretations of "The Eve of St. Agnes." Englewood Cliffs: Prentice, 1971.

Mades, Leonard. The Armor and the Brocade: A Study of Don Quijote and The Courtier. New York: Americas, 1968.

Traversi, Derek. The Canterbury Tales: A Reading. Newark: U of Delaware P, 1983.

4.5.24. A book published before 1900

When citing a book published before 1900, you may omit the name of the publisher and use a comma, instead of a colon, after the place of publication.

Dewey, John. The Study of Ethics: A Syllabus. Ann Arbor, 1894.

Udall, John. The Combate between Christ and the Devil: Four Sermones on the Temptations of Christ. London, 1589.

4.5.25. A book without stated publication information or pagination

When a book does not indicate the publisher, the place or date of publication, or the pagination, supply as much of the missing information as you can, using brackets to show that it did not come from the source:

New York: U of Gotham P, [1983].

If the date can only be approximated, put it after a *c.*, for *circa* 'around' ([c. 1983]). If you are uncertain about the accuracy of the information you are supplying, add a question mark ([1983?]). If you cannot supply any information, use the following abbreviations:

n.p.	no place of publication given
n.p.	no publisher given
n.d.	no date of publication given
n. pag.	no pagination given

Inserted before the colon, the abbreviation *n.p.* indicates *no place*; after the colon it indicates *no publisher. N. pag.* explains the absence of page references in citations of the work.

No place

N.p.: U of Gotham P, 1983.

No publisher

New York: n.p., 1983.

No date

New York: U of Gotham P, n.d.

No pagination

New York: U of Gotham P, 1983. N. pag.

Malachi, Zvi, ed. Proceedings of the International Conference on Literary and Linguistic Computing. [Tel Aviv]: [Fac. of Humanities, Tel Aviv U], n.d.

Photographic View Album of Cambridge. [England]: n.p., n.d. N. pag.

4.5.26. An unpublished dissertation

Place the title of an unpublished dissertation in quotation marks;

do not underline it. Then write the descriptive label *Diss.*, preceded and followed by two spaces, and add the name of the degree-granting university, followed by a comma, a space, and the year.

Boyle, Anthony T. "The Epistemological Evolution of Renaissance Utopian Literature: 1516-1657." Diss. New York U, 1983.

Johnson, Nancy Kay. "Cultural and Psychosocial Determinants of Health and Illness." Diss. U of Washington, 1980.

For citing a dissertation abstract published in *Dissertation Abstracts* or *Dissertation Abstracts International*, see 4.7.12. For documenting other unpublished writing, see 4.8.15.

4.5.27. A published dissertation

Treat a published dissertation like a book, but add pertinent dissertation information and, if the work has been published by University Microfilms International (UMI), the order number.

Brewda, Lee Aaron. A Semantically-Based Verb Valence Analysis of Old Saxon. Diss. Princeton U, 1981. Ann Arbor: UMI, 1982. 8203236.

Dietze, Rudolf F. Ralph Ellison: The Genesis of an Artist. Diss. U Erlangen-Nürnberg, 1982. Erlanger Beiträge zur Sprach- und Kunstwissenschaft 70. Nürnberg: Carl, 1982.

Wendriner, Karl Georg. Der Einfluss von Goethes Wilhelm Meister auf das Drama der Romantiker. Diss. U Bonn, 1907. Leipzig: privately printed, 1907.

4.6. Citing articles in periodicals: Information required

4.6.1. General guidelines

Periodicals are publications that appear regularly at fixed intervals. They include newspapers, magazines, and scholarly journals. An entry for an article in a periodical, like an entry for a book, has three main divisions: author, title of the article, and publication information. For scholarly journals the publication information generally includes the journal title, the volume number, the year of publication, and the inclusive page numbers of the article cited.

Booth, Wayne C. "Kenneth Burke's Way of Knowing." Critical Inquiry 1 (1974): 1-22.

Sometimes, however, additional information is required. Citations normally give the information in the following order:

1. Author's name
2. Title of the article
3. Name of the periodical
4. Series number or name
5. Volume number (for a scholarly journal)
6. Date of publication
7. Page numbers

Sections 4.6.2–8 give general recommendations for citing these items of information, and section 4.7 provides examples.

4.6.2. Author's name

Take the author's name from the beginning or the end of the article and follow the recommendations for citing names of authors of books (4.4.2).

4.6.3. Title of the article

Give the title of the article in full, enclosed in quotation marks (not underlined). Unless the title has its own concluding punctuation (e.g., a question mark), put a period before the closing quotation mark. Follow the recommendations for titles given in 2.5.

4.6.4. Name of the periodical

When citing a periodical, omit any introductory article but otherwise give the name, underlined, as it appears on the title page (*William and Mary Quarterly*, not *The William and Mary Quarterly*). Give the city or institution in square brackets to locate an unfamiliar journal or to distinguish a periodical from another with the same name. For newspaper titles, see 4.7.1.

4.6.5. Series number or name

If you list a periodical that has appeared in more than one series, state the number or name of the series after the journal title (see 4.7.6).

4.6.6. Volume number

Give the volume number for a scholarly journal (4.7.3) but not a newspaper (4.7.1) or a magazine (4.7.2). Your instructor or a librarian will help you if you are uncertain whether a periodical is a magazine or a scholarly journal. If any doubt remains, you may include the volume number. Do not precede the number with the word *volume* or the abbreviation *vol.* Although published several times a year (four issues is common), most scholarly journals paginate each annual volume continuously (see 4.7.3). Those that do page issues independently, however, require issue numbers as well as volume numbers (see 4.7.4), and some journals use issue numbers alone and do not have volume numbers (see 4.7.5).

4.6.7. Date of publication

Leave a space after the volume number and give the year of publication, in parentheses, followed by a colon, a space, and the inclusive page numbers of the article.

College Literature 8 (1981): 85-87.

In citing newspapers and magazines, omit volume and issue numbers and give the date instead, followed by a colon, a space, and the page number(s). Abbreviate all months except May, June, and July.

Folio Jan. 1980: 29-31.

Publishers Weekly 19 Feb. 1982: 6-7.

To cite editions of newspapers, see 4.7.1.

4.6.8. Page numbers

Using the rules for writing inclusive numbers (see 2.4.6), give the pages for the complete article, not just the pages used. (Specific page references appear parenthetically at appropriate places in your text; see ch. 5.) Write the page reference for the first page exactly as shown in the source (198–232, A32–34, 28/WETA–29, TV-15–18, lxii–lxv). A period follows the page numbers, concluding the entry.

When an article is not printed on consecutive pages—if, for example, it begins on page 6, then skips to page 10, and continues on page 22—write only the first page number and a plus sign, leaving no intervening space (6+).

McDonald, Kim. "New Materials That Conduct
    Electricity without Resistance Astound

Physicists." <u>Chronicle of Higher Education</u> 18 Mar. 1987: 1+.

To cite section numbers of newspapers, see 4.7.1.

4.7. Sample entries: Articles in periodicals

The following examples illustrate the recommendations in 4.6.

4.7.1. An article from a newspaper

In citing a newspaper, give the name as it appears on the masthead but omit any introductory article (*New York Times*, not *The New York Times*). If the city of publication is not included in the name of a locally published newspaper, add it in square brackets, not underlined, after the name (*Star-Ledger* [Newark, NJ]). For nationally published newspapers (e.g., *USA Today*, *Wall Street Journal*, *Chronicle of Higher Education*) you may omit the city of publication. Next, give the complete date—day, month (abbreviated), and year. Do not give the volume and issue numbers even if they are listed.

Because different editions of the same newspaper contain different material, specify the edition (if one is given on the masthead), preceded by a comma and a space, after the date:

Fuerbringer, Jonathan. "Budgetary Rhythms." <u>New York Times</u> 20 Mar. 1987, late ed.: A8.

or

Fuerbringer, Jonathan. "Budgetary Rhythms." <u>New York Times</u> 20 Mar. 1987, natl. ed.: 7

If each section is paginated separately, indicate the appropriate section number or letter. Determining how to indicate a section, however, can sometimes be complicated. The *New York Times*, for example, currently designates sections in three distinct ways, depending on the day of the week. On Monday through Friday, there are normally four sections, labeled *A*, *B*, *C*, and *D* and paginated separately, with each page number preceded by the section letter (A1, B1, C5, D3). On Saturday, the paper is not divided into specific sections, and pagination is continuous from the first page to the last. (The daily national edition follows the same practice.) Finally, the Sunday edition contains several individually paged sections (travel, arts and leisure, book reviews, business, sports, magazine, and others), designated not by letters but by numbers (Section 4), which do not appear as parts of the page numbers. Each system calls for a different method of indicating section and page.

If the newspaper is not divided into sections, give the page number after the date (and the edition, if one is stated on the masthead), a colon, and a space (see sample entry for Dalin). If the pagination includes a section designation, give the page number as it appears (C1; see sample entries for Schreiner and Tucker). If the section designation is not part of the pagination, put a comma after the date (and, if any, the edition) and add the abbreviation *sec.*, the appropriate letter or number, a colon, and the page number (see sample entry for Greeley).

Dalin, Damon. "A $7 Greeting Card? Yes, but Listen to the Melody It Will Play for You." Wall Street Journal 10 May 1983, eastern ed.: 37.

Greeley, Andrew. "Today's Morality Play: The Sitcom." New York Times 17 May 1987, late ed., sec. 2: 1+.

Schreiner, Tim. "Future Is A) Dim or B) Bright (Pick One)." USA Today 2 June 1983: 3A.

Tucker, Cynthia. "Education Stays on Top of Southerners' Agenda." Atlanta Constitution 21 Mar. 1987: 19A.

Wheeler, David L. "Artificial-Intelligence Researchers Develop Electronic 'Tutors' to Aid Learning Process." Chronicle of Higher Education 20 May 1987: 6-8.

4.7.2. An article from a magazine

In citing a magazine published every week or every two weeks, give the complete date (beginning with the day and abbreviating the month). Do not give the volume and issue numbers even if they are listed.

Prince, Dinah. "Marriage in the '80s." New York 1 June 1987: 30-38.

Walsh, John. "U.S.-Japan Study Aim Is Education Reform." Science 16 Jan. 1987: 274-75.

In citing a magazine published every month or every two months, give the month(s) and year. Do not give the volume and issue numbers even if they are listed.

Ferrara, Jerry L. "Why Vultures Make Good Neighbors." National Wildlife June-July 1987: 16-20.

Frazer, Lance. "Yours, Mine, or Ours: Who Owns the Moon?" Space World Nov. 1986: 24-26.

Lamb, Douglas H., and Glenn D. Reeder. "Reliving Golden Days." Psychology Today June 1986: 22+.

Nichols, Annabel. "A Tale of Two Brownstones."

Architectural Digest Feb. 1987: 96+.

Rogers, Peter. "Water: Not as Cheap as You Think." Technology Review Nov.-Dec. 1986: 30+.

4.7.3. An article in a scholarly journal with continuous pagination

Scholarly journals, usually appearing no more than four times a year, publish learned articles containing original research and original interpretations of data and texts. Their intended audience is not general readers but professionals and students. The research you do for your papers will inevitably lead you to consult scholarly journals.

A bibliographic reference to an article in a scholarly journal typically gives the name and volume number of the journal after the author's name and the title of the article. Take the title and volume number directly from the journal's cover, which may also include an issue number (Number 3) and the year preceded by a month (May 1987) or a season (Fall 1986). You may ignore the issue number and the month or season if the article you are citing appears in a journal that paginates continuously throughout the volume (i.e., if the first issue ends on page 130, the second issue begins on page 131, etc.). In citing such journals, give the volume number alone followed by the year of publication (in parentheses), a colon, and the inclusive page numbers. Suppose, for example, that you wish to cite the article "Bernini and Roman *Commedie Ridicolose*," by Jackson I. Cope, published in March 1987 in the second issue of volume 102 of the scholarly journal *PMLA*. The cover of that issue includes this publication information—"Volume 102, Number 2, March 1987"—but since *PMLA* is one of the many journals that page continuously by volume, omit the issue number and the month from your entry.

Cope, Jackson I. "Bernini and Roman Commedie Ridicolose." PMLA 102 (1987): 177-86.

Anyone reading this entry can find the source by locating the annual volume and turning directly to the appropriate pages for the article.

Brock, Dan W. "The Value of Prolonging Human Life." Philosophical Studies 50 (1986): 401-26.

Réger, Zita. "The Functions of Imitation in Child Language." Applied Psycholinguistics 7 (1986): 323-52.

Santley, Robert S. "The Political Economy of the Aztec Empire." Journal of Anthropological Research 41 (1985): 327-37.

4.7.4. An article in a scholarly journal that pages each issue separately

For a journal that does not number pages continuously throughout a volume but begins each issue on page 1, you must include the issue number to identify the source. Add a period and the issue number directly after the volume number, without any intervening space (14.2, signifying volume 14, issue 2; 10.3–4, for volume 10, issues 3 and 4 combined).

Barthelme, Frederick. "Architecture." Kansas Quarterly 13.3-4 (1981): 77-80.

Baum, Rosalie Murphy. "Alcoholism and Family Abuse in Maggie and The Bluest Eye." Mosaic 19.3 (1986): 91-105.

Winks, Robin W. "The Sinister Oriental Thriller: Fiction and the Asian Scene." Journal of Popular Culture 19.2 (1985): 49-61.

4.7.5. An article in a scholarly journal that uses only issue numbers

In citing a journal that uses only issue numbers, treat the issue number as you would a volume number.

Bowering, George. "Baseball and the Canadian Imagination." Canadian Literature 108 (1986): 115-24.

Samaan, Angele Botros. "Death and the Death Penalty in More's Utopia and Some Other Utopian Novels." Moreana 90 (1986): 5-15.

4.7.6. An article from a journal with more than one series

In citing a journal with numbered series, write the number (an arabic digit with the appropriate ordinal suffix: 2nd, 3rd, 4th, etc.) and the abbreviation *ser.* between the journal title and the volume number (see sample entry for Jackson). For a journal divided into a new series and an original series, indicate the series with *ns* or *os*, skip a space, and give the volume number (see sample entry for Gass).

Gass, William H. "Some Snapshots from the Soviet Zone." Kenyon Review ns 8.4 (1986): 1-43.

Jackson, Harvey H. "Hugh Bryan and the Evangelical Movement in Colonial South Carolina." William and Mary Quarterly 3rd ser. 43 (1986): 594-614.

4.7.7. An editorial

If you are citing a signed editorial, begin with the author's name, give the title, and then add the descriptive label *Editorial,* neither underlined nor enclosed in quotation marks. Conclude with the appropriate publication information. If the editorial is unsigned, begin with the title and continue in the same way.

```
Evans, Harold.  "Free Speech and Free Air."
     Editorial.  U.S. News and World Report 11
     May 1987: 82.
"A Fee, Not a Ban, on Audio Progress."
     Editorial.  New York Times 24 May 1987,
     late ed., sec. 4: 16.
```

4.7.8. An anonymous article

If no author's name is given for the article you are citing, begin the entry with the title and alphabetize by title.

```
"Drunkproofing Automobiles."  Time 6 Apr. 1987:
     37.
"A Traffic Ban Drives Rome Crazy."  Newsweek 16
     Mar. 1987: 47.
```

4.7.9. A letter to the editor

To identify a letter to the editor, add the descriptive label *Letter* after the name of the author, but do not underline the word or place it in quotation marks.

```
Levin, Harry.  Letter.  Partisan Review 47
     (1980): 320.
```

If an author has replied to a letter, identify the response as "Reply to letter of . . . ," and add the name of the writer of the initial letter. Do not underline this information or place it in quotation marks.

Patai, Daphne. Reply to letter of Erwin Hester. PMLA 98 (1983): 257-58.

4.7.10. A review

In citing a review, give the reviewer's name and the title of the review (if there is one); then write *Rev. of* (neither underlined nor placed in quotation marks), the title of the work reviewed, a comma, the word *by*, and the name of the author. If the work of an editor or translator is under review, use *ed.* or *trans.* instead of *by.* For the review of a performance, add pertinent information about the production (see sample entry for Anderson). Conclude with the name of the periodical and the rest of the publication information.

If the review is titled but unsigned, begin the entry with the title of the review and alphabetize by that title (see sample entry for "The Cooling of an Admiration"). If the review is neither titled nor signed, begin the entry with *Rev. of* and alphabetize under the title of the work being reviewed (see sample entry for *Anthology of Danish Literature*).

Anderson, Jack. Rev. of Don Quixote. American Ballet Theater. Metropolitan Opera House, New York. New York Times 30 May 1987, late ed.: 13.

Rev. of Anthology of Danish Literature, ed. F. J. Billeskov Jansen and P. M. Mitchell. Times Literary Supplement 7 July 1972: 785.

"The Cooling of an Admiration." Rev. of Pound/Joyce: The Letters of Ezra Pound to James Joyce, with Pound's Essays on Joyce, ed. Forrest Read. Times Literary Supplement 6 Mar. 1969: 239-40.

Craft, Robert. "The Maestro on the Market." Rev. of Understanding Toscanini: How He Became an American Culture-God and Helped Create a New Audience for Old Music, by Joseph Horowitz. New York Review of Books 9 Apr. 1987: 20-22.

Edwards, R. Dudley. Rev. of The Dissolution of the Religious Orders in Ireland under Henry VIII, by Brendan Bradshaw. Renaissance Quarterly 29 (1976): 401-03.

Hall, Lucia K. B. Rev. of God and the New Physics, by Paul Davies. Humanist Nov.-Dec. 1986: 39.

4.7.11. An article whose title contains a quotation or a title within quotation marks

If the title of the article you are citing contains a quotation or a title within quotation marks, use single quotation marks around the quotation or the shorter title (see 2.5.4).

Carrier, Warren. "Commonplace Costumes and Essential Gaudiness: Wallace Stevens' 'The Emperor of Ice-Cream.'" College Literature 1 (1974): 230-35.

Duncan-Jones, E. E. "Moore's 'A Kiss à l'Antique' and Keats's 'Ode on a Grecian Urn.'" Notes and Queries ns 28 (1981): 316-17.

Nitzsche, Jane Chance. "'As swete as is the roote of lycorys, or any cetewale': Herbal Imagery in Chaucer's Miller's Tale." Chaucer Newsletter 2.1 (1980): 6-8.

4.7.12. An abstract from *Dissertation Abstracts* or *Dissertation Abstracts International*

Beginning with volume 30 (1969), *Dissertation Abstracts* (*DA*) became *Dissertation Abstracts International* (*DAI*). From volume 27 to volume 36, *DA* and *DAI* were paginated in two series: *A* for humanities and social sciences, *B* for the sciences. With volume 37, *DAI* added a third separately paginated section: *C* for abstracts of European dissertations. Identify the degree-granting institution at the end of a *DA* or *DAI* entry (for citing dissertations themselves, see 4.5.26–27).

Gans, Eric L. "The Discovery of Illusion: Flaubert's Early Works, 1835-1837." DA 27 (1967): 3046A. Johns Hopkins U.

Johnson, Nancy Kay. "Cultural and Psychosocial Determinants of Health and Illness." DAI 40 (1980): 4235B. U of Washington.

Norris, Christine Lynn. "Literary Allusion in the Tales of Isak Dinesen." DAI 43 (1982): 453A. U of California, San Diego.

4.7.13. A serialized article

To cite a serialized article or a series of related articles published in more than one issue of a periodical, include all bibliographic information in one entry if each installment has the same author and title.

Gillespie, Gerald. "Novella, Nouvelle, Novelle, Short Novel? A Review of Terms." Neophilologus 51 (1967): 117-27, 225-30.

Meserole, Harrison T., and James M. Rambeau. "Articles on American Literature Appearing in Current Periodicals." American Literature 52 (1981): 688-705; 53 (1981): 164-80, 348-59.

If the installments bear different titles, list each one separately. You may include a brief description at the end of the entry to indicate that the article is part of a series.

Gottlieb, Martin. "Pressure and Compromise Saved Times Square Project." New York Times 10 Mar. 1984, late ed.: 25. Pt. 2 of a series begun on 9 Mar. 1984.

---. "Times Square Development Plan: A Lesson in Politics and Power." New York Times 9 Mar. 1984, late ed.: B1. Pt. 1 of a series.

4.8. Sample entries: Other sources

4.8.1. Computer software

An entry for a commercially produced computer program should contain the following information: the writer of the program, if known; the title of the program, underlined; the version of the program, preceded by the abbreviation *vers.*; the descriptive label *Computer software*, neither underlined nor enclosed in quotation marks; the distributor; and the year of publication. Put a period after each item except the distributor, which is followed by a comma. At the end of the entry add any other pertinent information—for example, the operating system for which the program is designed (PC-DOS 2.10, CP/M 2.2); the number of kilobytes, or units of memory (8KB); and the form of the program (cartridge, cassette, disk). Separate these items with commas and conclude the entry with a period.

Rosenberg, Victor, et al. Pro-Cite. Vers. 1.3. Computer software. Personal Bibliographic Software, 1987. IBM PC-DOS 2.0, 256KB, disk.

Shapiro, Marvin, and Ted Salzman. Bibliography Generator. Computer software. Educational Activities, 1987. PC-DOS 2.11, 256KB, disk.

Soldan, Theodore J., and James D. Spain. Population Growth. Computer software. Conduit, 1984.

4.8.2. Material from a computer service

Treat material obtained from a computer service—such as BRS, Dialog, or Mead—like other printed material, but add a reference to the service at the end of the entry. Give the publication information as provided by the service, the name of the service, and the accession or identifying numbers within the service.

Schomer, Howard. "South Africa: Beyond Fair Employment." Harvard Business Review May-June 1983: 145+. Dialog file 122, item 119425 833160.

"Turner, Barbara Bush." <u>American Men and Women of Science</u>. 15th ed. Bowker, 1983. Dialog file 236, item 0107406.

```
File122:Harvard Business Review - 1971-84,Jan/Feb
(Copr. Harvard 1984)

119425          833160          **COMPLETE TEXT AVAILABLE**
   South Africa: Beyond Fair Employment
   Schomer, Howard - Howard Schomer Associates - United Church of Christ
   HARVARD BUSINESS REVIEW, May/Jun 1983, p. 145

   TEXT:
   Executives of companies with interests in South Africa have known for
some time that neutrality toward the government's policy of apartheid is at
least irresponsible, if not downright dishonest. Few actually agree with
the notion that enshrining white supremacy as a constitutional principle is
a defensible political course.
   And so they've done something about it. When the government of Prime
Minister Pieter Botha allowed limited yet independent black unions in 1979,
for example, some companies immediately began to negotiate with
representatives of blacks and bypassed the government-supported labor
organizations, which are dominated by whites. Fully 30% of the 400 U.S.
companies with affiliates or subsidiaries in South Africa have committed
themselves to racial equality in their operations, in accordance with six
principles promulgated in 1977 by the Reverend Leon Sullivan, a black
social reformer who has become a member of the board of directors of
General Motors (for more details on the Sullivan initiative, see the ruled
insert).
   But are such actions by companies enough? Absolutely not. Events of the
last few years cause knowledgeable corporate executives to despair whether
the white rulers of South Africa will be able to move swiftly enough toward
equal rights for all. No longer can they think that the problem will simply
go away or that the government can indefinitely contain the black drive for
equality. The much-heralded initiative to allow independent black unions,
taken after a 1976 police assault on unarmed demonstrators in Soweto that
resulted in 600 deaths, 6,000 arrests, and hundreds of banning orders, has
been followed in 1980 to 1982 by a climate of renewed repression in which:
   More than a dozen trade union leaders have been held for long periods
without trial for questioning.
   Ten prisoners have reportedly committed suicide while being held without
charge or trial under the stringent security laws.
   An unprecedented court inquiry into the mysterious death of a white
prisoner, Dr. Neil Aggett, while formally exonerating prison officials,
pointed up the kinds of torture the government uses as standard practice.
   Black political groups, like the African National Congress, have been
systematically banned, and white workers for black unions, like Barbara
Anne Hogan, have been sentenced to ten years imprisonment for high treason.
```

The beginning of an article from Harvard Business Review *as retrieved from Dialog. Entering the appropriate file number (122) yields a note on the holdings available. Having searched the entire holdings for appropriate terms, the system retrieved this article.*

4.8.3. Material from an information service

Treat material obtained from an information service—such as ERIC (Educational Resources Information Center) or NTIS (National Technical Information Service)—like other printed material, but add a reference to the service at the end of the entry. If the material was published previously, give the full details of its original publication, followed by the name of the service and the identifying number within the service.

Phillips, June K., ed. Action for the '80s: A Political, Professional, and Public Program for Foreign Language Education. Skokie: Natl. Textbook, 1981. ERIC ED 197 599.

Spolsky, Bernard. Navajo Language Maintenance: Six-Year-Olds in 1969. Navajo Reading Study Prog. Rept. 5. Albuquerque: U of New Mexico, 1969. ERIC ED 043 004.

If the material was not previously published, treat its distribution by the information service as the mode of publication.

Streiff, Paul R. Some Criteria for Designing Evaluation of TESOL Programs. ERIC, 1970. ED 040 385.

No place of publication is cited for materials distributed by the ERIC Document Reproduction Service (EDRS), since the location of this government-sponsored service changes.

4.8.4. Television and radio programs

The information for an entry for a television or radio program usually appears in the following order: the title of the program, underlined; the network (PBS); the local station on which you saw or heard the program and the city (KETC, St. Louis); and the broadcast date. Where appropriate, the title of the episode, in quotation marks, should precede the title of the program, and the title of the series, neither underlined nor enclosed in quotation marks, should appear after the program (see sample entry for "Agnes, the Indomitable de Mille"). Use a comma between the station and the city, periods after all other items. For the inclusion of other information that may be pertinent (e.g., director, narrator, producer), see the sample entries.

"Agnes, the Indomitable de Mille." Narr. Agnes de Mille. Prod. Judy Kinberg. Dir. Merrill Brockway. Dance in America. Exec. prod. Jac Venza. Great Performances. PBS. WGBH, Boston. 8 May 1987.

Candide. By Leonard Bernstein. Book by Hugh Wheeler. Lyrics by Richard Wilbur, Stephen Sondheim, and John Latouche. Dir. Harold Prince. With Erie Mills, David Eisler, and John Lankston. Cond. Scott Bergeson. New York City Opera. PBS. WNET, New York. 12 Nov. 1986. Based on Voltaire's Candide.

The First Americans. Narr. Hugh Downs. Writ. and prod. Craig Fisher. NBC News Special. KNBC, Los Angeles. 21 Mar. 1968.

Lucia di Lammermoor. By Gaetano Donizetti. With Edita Gruberova and Neil Shicoff. Lyric Opera of Chicago. Nuveen-Lyric Opera of Chicago Radio Network. WFMT, Chicago. 20 June 1987.

If your reference is primarily to the work of a particular individual, cite that person's name before the title.

Dickens, Charles. The Life and Adventures of Nicholas Nickleby. Adapt. David Edgar. Dir. Trevor Nunn and John Caird. With Roger Rees and Emily Richard. Royal Shakespeare Co. Mobil Showcase Network. WNEW, New York. 10-13 Jan. 1983.

Welles, Orson, dir. War of the Worlds. Writ. Howard Koch. Mercury Theatre on the Air. CBS Radio. WCBS, New York. 30 Oct. 1938. Based on H. G. Wells's War of the Worlds.

See 4.8.11 for interviews on radio and television programs; see also 4.8.5 for recordings and 4.8.7 for performances.

4.8.5. Recordings

In an entry for a commercially available recording, the person cited first (e.g., the composer, conductor, or performer) will depend on the desired emphasis. List the title of the record or tape (or the titles of the works included), the artist(s), the manufacturer, the catalog number, and the year of issue (if the year is unknown, write *n.d.*). Commas follow the manufacturer and the number; periods follow other items. If you are using a tape recording, indicate the medium (Audiotape), neither underlined nor placed in quotation marks, immediately after the title (see sample entries for Eliot and Wilgus). Include physical characteristics at the end of the entry if the information is relevant or if the recording is not readily available (see sample entry for Wilgus).

In general, underline record titles (*Romances for Saxophone*), but do not underline or put in quotation marks the titles of musical compositions identified only by form, number, and key (see 2.5.2 as well as the sample entry for Beethoven). You may wish to indicate, in addition to the year of issue, the actual date of recording (see sample entries for Ellington and Holiday).

Beethoven, Ludwig van. Symphony no. 5 in C and Symphony no. 6 in F. Cond. Vladimir Ashkenazy. Philharmonia Orch. London, LDR-72015, 1982.

Berlioz, Hector. Symphonie fantastique, op. 14. Cond. Herbert von Karajan. Berlin Philharmonic. Deutsche Grammophon, 2530 597, 1975.

Ellington, Duke, cond. Duke Ellington Orch. First Carnegie Hall Concert. Rec. 23 Jan. 1943. Prestige, P-34004, 1977.

Holiday, Billie. "God Bless the Child." Rec. 9 May 1941. Billie Holiday: The Golden Years. Columbia, C3L 21, 1962.

Joplin, Scott. Treemonisha. With Carmen Balthrop, Betty Allen, and Curtis Rayam. Cond. Gunther Schuller. Houston Grand Opera Orch. and Chorus. Deutsche Grammophon, S-2707 083, 1975.

Lloyd Webber, Andrew. Cats. With Elaine Page and Brian Blessed. Cond. David Firman. Geffen, 2GHS 2017, 1981. Based on T. S. Eliot's Old Possum's Book of Practical Cats.

Marsalis, Branford, soprano saxophone. "The Old Castle." Pictures at an Exhibition. By Modest Mussorgsky. Romances for Saxophone. Cond. Andrew Litton. English Chamber Orch. CBS, MT-42122, 1986.

Prokofiev, Sergei. Symphony no. 1 in D, op. 25; Suite from Love for Three Oranges, op. 33a; Lieutenant Kijé, Symphonic Suite, op. 60. Cond. Lorin Maazel. Orch. National de France. CBS, IM-39557, 1985.

Purcell, Henry. Dido and Aeneas. With Jessye Norman and Thomas Allen. Cond. Raymond Leppard. English Chamber Orch. and Chorus. Philips, 416 299-1, 1986.

Sondheim, Stephen. Sunday in the Park with George. With Mandy Patinkin and Bernadette Peters. Cond. Paul Gemignani. RCA, HBC1-5042, 1984.

Treat a recording of the spoken word as you would a musical recording. Begin with the speaker, the writer, or the production director, depending on the desired emphasis.

Eliot, T. S. Old Possum's Book of Practical Cats. Audiotape. Read by John Gielgud and Irene Worth. Caedmon, CP 1713, 1983.

Frost, Robert. "The Road Not Taken." Robert Frost Reads His Poetry. Caedmon, TC 1060, 1956.

Lehmann, Lotte. *Lotte Lehmann Reading German Poetry*. Caedmon, TC 1072, 1958.

Murrow, Edward R. *Year of Decision: 1943*. Columbia, CPS-3872, 1957.

Shakespeare, William. *Othello*. Dir. John Dexter. With Laurence Olivier, Maggie Smith, Frank Finley, and Derek Jacobi. RCA, VDM-100, 1964.

Welles, Orson, dir. *War of the Worlds*. Writ. Howard Koch. Mercury Theatre on the Air. Rec. 30 Oct. 1938. Evolution, 4001, 1969. Based on H. G. Wells's *War of the Worlds*.

Do not underline or enclose in quotation marks the title of a private or archival recording or tape. Include the date recorded (if known), the location and identifying number of the recording, and the physical characteristics (if ascertainable).

Wilgus, D. K. Southern Folk Tales. Audiotape. Rec. 23-25 Mar. 1965. U of California, Los Angeles, Archives of Folklore. B.76.82. 7 1/2 ips, 7" reel.

In citing the jacket notes, libretto, or other material accompanying a recording, give the author's name, the title of the material (if any), and a description of the material (Jacket notes, Libretto). Then provide the usual bibliographic information for a recording.

Colette. Libretto. *L'enfant et les sortilèges*. Music by Maurice Ravel. With Suzanne Danco and Hugues Cuenod. Cond. Ernest Ansermet.

Orch. de la Suise Romande. Richmond-London, SR 33086, n.d.

Collins, Judy. Jacket notes. Antonia Brico, cond. Mostly Mozart Orch. Symphony no. 35 in D and Overtures to The Marriage of Figaro, The Magic Flute, and Don Giovanni. By Wolfgang A. Mozart. Columbia, M33888, 1976.

Lawrence, Vera Brodsky. "Scott Joplin and Treemonisha." Libretto. Treemonisha. By Scott Joplin. Deutsche Grammophon, S-2707 083, 1975. 10-12.

Lewiston, David. Jacket notes. The Balinese Gamelan: Music from the Morning of the World. Nonesuch Explorer Ser., H-2015, n.d.

4.8.6. Films, filmstrips, slide programs, and videotapes

A film citation usually begins with the title, underlined, and includes the director, the distributor, and the year. You may include other data that seem pertinent: information such as the writer, performers, and producer would follow the title; physical characteristics, such as the size and length of the film, would go after the date.

It's a Wonderful Life. Dir. Frank Capra. With James Stewart, Donna Reed, Lionel Barrymore, and Thomas Mitchell. RKO, 1946.

What Makes Rabbit Run? Dir. David Chesire and R. Eaton. Centre Productions, 1985. 16 mm, 29 min.

If you are citing the contribution of a particular individual, begin with that person's name.

Chaplin, Charles, dir. Modern Times. With Chaplin and Paulette Goddard. United Artists, 1936.

Jhabvala, Ruth Prawer, screenwriter. A Room with a View. Dir. James Ivory. Prod. Ismail Merchant. Original score by Richard Robbins. With Maggie Smith, Denholm Elliott, and Helena Bonham-Carter. Cinecom Intl. Films, 1985. Based on E. M. Forster's A Room with a View.

Mifune, Toshiro, actor. Rashomon. Dir. Akira Kurosawa. With Machiko Kyo. Daiei, 1950.

Rota, Nino, composer. Giulietta degli spiriti [Juliet of the Spirits]. Dir. Federico Fellini. With Giulietta Masina. Rizzoli, 1965.

In citing a filmstrip, slide program, or videotape, include the medium, neither underlined nor enclosed in quotation marks, immediately after the title and then give the usual bibliographic information for films.

Alcohol Use and Its Medical Consequences: A Comprehensive Teaching Program for Biomedical Education. Slide program. Dev. Project Cork, Dartmouth Medical School. Milner-Fenwick, 1982. 46 slides.

Alzheimer's Disease. Videocassette. Prod. Hospital Satellite Network. American Journal of Nursing, 1985. 28 min.

Special Effects. Videocassette. Writ. and prod. Charles Halpern. Dir. Charles Rudnick. U of California Extension Media Center, 1985. 58 min.

Survey of the Animal Kingdom: The Invertebrates. Sound filmstrip. By J. L. Wassink and C. R. Belinsky. Educational Images, 1985. 4 filmstrips, 4 audiocassettes.

4.8.7. Performances

An entry for a performance (play, opera, ballet, concert) usually begins with the title, contains information similar to that for a film (see 4.8.6), and concludes with the theater and city, separated by a comma and followed by a period, and the date of the performance.

Candide. By Leonard Bernstein. Book by Hugh Wheeler. Lyrics by Richard Wilbur, Stephen Sondheim, and John Latouche. Dir. Harold Prince. With Erie Mills, David Eisler, and John Lankston. Cond. Scott Bergeson. New York City Opera, New York. 12 Nov. 1986.

Cats. By Andrew Lloyd Webber. Dir. Trevor Nunn. New London Theatre, London. 11 May 1981. Based on T. S. Eliot's Old Possum's Book of Practical Cats.

La Fanciulla del West. By Giacomo Puccini. Dir. Patrick Bakman. Cond. Stefan Minde. With Marilyn Zschau and Vladimir Popov. Portland Opera Assn. Civic Auditorium, Portland, OR. 17 Mar. 1983.

Hamlet. By William Shakespeare. Dir. John Gielgud. With Richard Burton. Shubert Theatre, Boston. 4 Mar. 1964.

If you are citing the contribution of a particular individual, begin with that person's name.

Baryshnikov, Mikhail, chor. Don Quixote. With Martine van Hamel and Kevin McKenzie. American Ballet Theater. Metropolitan Opera House, New York. 26 May 1986.

Caldwell, Sarah, dir. and cond. La Traviata. By Giuseppe Verdi. With Beverly Sills. Opera Co. of Boston. Orpheum Theatre, Boston. 4 Nov. 1972.

Ellington, Duke, cond. Duke Ellington Orch. Concert. Carnegie Hall, New York. 23 Jan. 1943.

Joplin, Scott. Treemonisha. Dir. Frank Corsaro. Cond. Gunther Schuller. With Carmen Balthrop, Betty Allen, and Curtis Rayam. Houston Grand Opera. Miller Theatre, Houston. 18 May 1975.

Lapine, James, dir. Sunday in the Park with George. By Stephen Sondheim. With Mandy Patinkin and Bernadette Peters. Booth Theatre, New York. 2 May 1984.

Shaw, Robert, cond. Atlanta Symphony Orch. Concert. Atlanta Arts Center, Atlanta. 14 Dec. 1981.

Wilson, August. Fences. Dir. Lloyd Richards. With James Earl Jones. Forty-Sixth Street Theatre, New York. 6 June 1987.

For broadcasts and telecasts of performances, see 4.8.4; for recordings of performances, see 4.8.5.

4.8.8. Musical compositions

In citing a musical composition, begin with the composer's name. Underline the title of an opera, a ballet, or instrumental music identified by name (*Symphonie fantastique*), but do not underline or put in quotation marks an instrumental composition identified only by form, number, and key.

Beethoven, Ludwig van. Symphony no. 7 in A, op. 92.

Berlioz, Hector. Symphonie fantastique, op. 14.

Wagner, Richard. Götterdämmerung.

Treat a published score, however, like a book. Give the title as it appears on the title page and underline it.

Beethoven, Ludwig van. Symphony No. 7 in A, Op. 92. Kalmus Miniature Orchestra Scores 7. New York: Kalmus, n.d.

See 4.8.5 for recordings of musical compositions, 4.8.4 for radio and television programs, and 4.8.7 for performances.

4.8.9. Works of art

In citing a work of art, state the artist's name first. In general, underline the title of a painting or sculpture. Name the institution housing the work (e.g., a museum), followed by a comma and the city.

Bernini, Gianlorenzo. Ecstasy of St. Teresa. Santa Maria della Vittoria, Rome.

Rembrandt van Rijn. Aristotle Contemplating the Bust of Homer. Metropolitan Museum of Art, New York.

If you use a photograph of the work, indicate not only the institution and the city but also the complete publication information for the work in which the photograph appears.

Cassatt, Mary. Mother and Child. Wichita Art Museum, Wichita. Slide 22 of American Painting: 1560-1913. By John Pearce. New York: McGraw, 1964.

Houdon, Jean-Antoine. Statue of Voltaire. Comédie Française, Paris. Illus. 51 in Literature through Art: A New Approach to French Literature. By Helmut A. Hatzfeld. New York: Oxford UP, 1952.

4.8.10. Letters

As bibliographic entries, letters fall into three general categories: (1) published letters, (2) letters in archives, and (3) letters received by the researcher. Treat a published letter like a work in a collection (see 4.5.8), adding the date of the letter and the number (if the editor has assigned one).

Thackeray, William Makepeace. "To George Henry Lewes." 6 Mar. 1848. Letter 452 in Letters and Private Papers of William Makepeace Thackeray. Ed. Gordon N. Ray. Vol. 2. Cambridge: Harvard UP, 1946. 353-54.

If you are citing more than one letter from a published collection, however, provide a single entry for the entire work and give individual citations in the text (see 4.5.10).

In citing an unpublished letter, follow the basic guidelines for manuscripts and typescripts (see 4.8.15) or for private and archival recordings and tapes (see 4.8.5).

Benton, Thomas Hart. Letter to Charles Fremont. 22 June 1847. John Charles Fremont Papers. Southwest Museum Library, Los Angeles.

Cite a letter that you yourself have received as follows:

Copland, Aaron. Letter to the author. 17 May 1982.

4.8.11. Interviews

The citation form for interviews depends on whether they were (1) published or recorded, (2) broadcast on radio or television, or (3) conducted by the researcher. Begin with the name of the person interviewed. If the interview is part of a publication, recording, or program, put the title, if any, in quotation marks; if the interview is the entire work, underline the title. If the interview is untitled, use the descriptive label *Interview*, neither underlined nor enclosed in quotation marks. (The interviewer's name may be included if known and pertinent; see sample entry for Lansbury.) Conclude with the usual bibliographic information required for the entry.

Fellini, Federico. "The Long Interview." Juliet of the Spirits. Ed. Tullio Kezich. Trans. Howard Greenfield. New York: Ballantine, 1966. 17-64.

Kundera, Milan. Interview. New York Times 18 Jan. 1982, late ed., sec. 3: 13+.

Lansbury, Angela. Interview. Off-Camera: Conversations with the Makers of Prime-Time Television. By Richard Levinson and William Link. New York: Plume-NAL, 1986. 72-86.

Morrison, Toni. Interview. All Things Considered. Natl. Public Radio. WNYC, New York. 16 Feb. 1986.

Wolfe, Tom. Interview. The Wrong Stuff: American Architecture. Videocassette. Dir. Tom Bettag. Carousel Films, 1983.

In citing a personally conducted interview, give the name of the interviewee, the kind of interview (Personal interview, Telephone interview), and the date.

Pei, I. M. Personal interview. 27 July 1983.

Poussaint, Alvin F. Telephone interview. 10 Dec. 1980.

4.8.12. Maps and charts

In general, treat a map or chart like an anonymous book, but add the appropriate descriptive label (Map, Chart).

Canada. Map. Chicago: Rand, 1987.

Grammar and Punctuation. Chart. Grand Haven: School Zone, 1980.

For additional guidance in citing such sources as dioramas, flash-cards, games, globes, kits, and models, see Eugene B. Fleischer, *A Style Manual for Citing Microform and Nonprint Media* (Chicago: ALA, 1978).

4.8.13. Cartoons

To cite a cartoon, state the cartoonist's name, the title of the cartoon (if any) in quotation marks, and the descriptive label *Cartoon*, neither underlined nor enclosed in quotation marks. Conclude with the usual publication information.

Booth, George. Cartoon. New Yorker 13 Apr. 1987: 25.

Trudeau, Garry. "Doonesbury." Cartoon. Star-Ledger [Newark, NJ] 27 May 1987: 25.

4.8.14. Lectures, speeches, and addresses

Give the speaker's name, the title of the lecture (if known) in quotation marks, the meeting and the sponsoring organization (if applicable), the location, and the date. If there is no title, use an appropriate descriptive label (Lecture, Address, Keynote speech), neither underlined nor enclosed in quotation marks.

Ciardi, John. Address. Opening General Sess.
NCTE Convention. Washington, 19 Nov. 1982.

Kristeva, Julia. "Healing and Truth in
Psychoanalysis." Div. on Psychological
Approaches to Literature. MLA Convention.
New York, 29 Dec. 1986.

4.8.15. Manuscripts and typescripts

In citing a manuscript or a typescript, state the author, the title or a description of the material (Notebook), the form of the material (ms. for manuscript, ts. for typescript), and any identifying number assigned to it. If a library or other research institution houses the material, give its name and location.

Chaucer, Geoffrey. The Canterbury Tales.
Harley ms. 7334. British Museum, London.

Smith, John. "Shakespeare's Dark Lady."
Unpublished essay, 1983.

Twain, Mark. Notebook 32, ts. Mark Twain
Papers. U of California, Berkeley.

4.8.16. Legal references

The citation of legal documents and law cases may be complicated. If your paper requires many such references, consult the most recent edition of *A Uniform System of Citation* (Cambridge: Harvard Law Rev. Assn.), an indispensable guide in this field.

In general, do not underline or enclose in quotation marks laws, acts, and similar documents in either the text or the list of works cited

(Declaration of Independence, Constitution of the United States, Taft-Hartley Act). Such works are usually cited by sections, with the year added if relevant. Although lawyers and legal scholars adopt many abbreviations in their citations, use only familiar abbreviations when writing for a more general audience (see ch. 6).

```
15 US Code.  Sec. 78j(b).  1964.

US Const.  Art. 1, sec. 1
```

Note that in references to the United States Code, often abbreviated *USC*, the title number precedes the code (12 USC, 15 USC). Alphabetize under *United States Code* even if you use the abbreviation. When including more than one reference to the code, list individual entries in numerical order.

Names of law cases are both abbreviated and shortened (Brown v. Board of Ed., for Oliver Brown versus Board of Education of Topeka, Kansas), but the first important word of each party is always spelled out. Unlike laws, names of cases are underlined in the text but not in bibliographic entries. In citing a case, include, in addition to the names of the first plaintiff and the first defendant, the volume, name (not underlined), and page (in that order) of the law report cited; the name of the court that decided the case; and the year in which it was decided. Once again, considerable abbreviation is the norm. The following citation, for example, refers to page 755 of volume 148 of the *United States Patent Quarterly*, dealing with the case of Stevens against the National Broadcasting Company, which was decided by the California Superior Court in 1966.

```
Stevens v. National Broadcasting Co.  148 USPQ
     755.  CA Super. Ct.  1966.
```

5. DOCUMENTING SOURCES

5.1. What to document

In writing your research paper, you must document everything that you borrow—not only direct quotations and paraphrases but also information and ideas. Of course, common sense as well as ethics should determine what you document. For example, you rarely need to give sources for familiar proverbs ("You can't judge a book by its cover"), well-known quotations ("We shall overcome"), or common knowledge ("George Washington was the first president of the United States"). But you must indicate the source of any appropriated material that readers might otherwise mistake for your own. (On note-taking and plagiarism, see 1.5 and 1.6, respectively.)

5.2. Parenthetical documentation and the list of works cited

The list of works cited at the end of your research paper plays an important role in your acknowledgment of sources (see ch. 4), but it does not in itself provide sufficiently detailed and precise documentation. You must indicate exactly what you have derived from each source and exactly where in that work you found the material. The most practical way to supply this information is to insert brief parenthetical acknowledgments in your paper wherever you incorporate another's words, facts, or ideas. Usually the author's last name and a page reference are enough to identify the source and the specific location from which you have borrowed material.

```
Ancient writers attributed the invention of the
monochord to Pythagoras in the sixth century BC
(Marcuse 197).
```

The parenthetical reference indicates that the information on the monochord comes from page 197 of the book by Marcuse included in the alphabetically arranged list of works cited that follows the text. Thus it enables the reader to find complete publication information for the source:

Marcuse, Sibyl. A Survey of Musical
    Instruments. New York: Harper, 1975.

The sample references in 5.5 offer recommendations for documenting many other kinds of sources.

5.3. Information required in parenthetical documentation

In determining the information needed to document sources accurately, keep the following guidelines in mind:

1. *References in the text must clearly point to specific sources in the list of works cited.* The information in the parenthetical reference, therefore, must match the corresponding information in the list. The reference typically begins with the name of the author (or whoever else begins the works cited entry, such as an editor, translator, speaker, or artist). When the list contains only one work by the author cited, you need give only the author's last name to identify the work (though you would, of course, have to indicate the first name as well, usually by an initial only, if two authors on the list had the same last name). If two or three names begin the entry, give the last name of each person listed. If the work has more than three authors, follow the form in the bibliographic entry: give the first author's last name followed by *et al.*, without any intervening punctuation (Edens et al.), or give all the last names. If there is a corporate author, use that name, or a shortened version of it (see 5.5.5); if the work is listed by title, use the title, or a shortened version (see 5.5.4); if the list contains more than one work by the author, add the cited title, or a shortened version, after the author's last name (see 5.5.6).

2. *Identify the location of the borrowed information as specifically as possible.* Give the relevant page number(s) (see 5.5.2) or, if citing from more than one volume of a multivolume work, the volume and page

number(s) (see 5.5.3). In references to literary works, it is helpful to give information other than, or in addition to, the page numbers—for example, the chapter, the book, the stanza, or the act, scene, and line (see 5.5.8). You may omit page numbers when citing one-page articles, articles in works arranged alphabetically (like encyclopedias), or, of course, nonprint sources (see 5.5.4).

5.4. Readability

Keep parenthetical references as brief—and as few—as clarity and accuracy permit. Give only the information needed to identify a source and do not add a parenthetical reference unnecessarily. Identify sources by author and, if necessary, title; do not use abbreviations such as *ed.*, *trans.*, or *comp.* after the name. If you are citing an entire work, for example, rather than a specific part of it, the author's name in the text may be the only documentation required. The statement "Booth has devoted an entire book to the subject" needs no parenthetical documentation if the list of works cited includes only one work by Booth. If, for the reader's convenience, you wished to name the book in your text, you could recast the sentence: "In *The Rhetoric of Fiction* Booth deals with this subject exclusively."

Remember that there is a direct relation between what you integrate into your text and what you place in parentheses. If, for example, you include an author's name in a sentence, you need not repeat it in the parenthetical page citation that follows. It will be clear that the reference is to the work of the author you have mentioned. The paired sentences below illustrate how to cite authors in the text to keep parenthetical references concise.

Author's name in text

Frye has argued this point before (178-85).

Author's name in reference

This point has been argued before (Frye 178-85).

Authors' names in text

Others, like Wellek and Warren (310-15), hold an opposite point of view.

Authors' names in reference

Others hold an opposite point of view (e.g., Wellek and Warren 310-15).

Author's name in text

Only Daiches has seen this relation (2: 776-77).

Author's name in reference

Only one critic has seen this relation (Daiches 2: 776-77).

Author's name in text

It may be true, as Robertson maintains, that "in the appreciation of medieval art the attitude of the observer is of primary importance . . ." (136).

Author's name in reference

It may be true that "in the appreciation of medieval art the attitude of the observer is of primary importance . . ." (Robertson 136).

To avoid interrupting the flow of your writing, place the parenthetical reference where a pause would naturally occur (preferably at the end of a sentence), as near as possible to the material it documents. The parenthetical reference precedes the punctuation mark that concludes the sentence, clause, or phrase containing the borrowed material.

In his Autobiography, Benjamin Franklin states that he prepared a list of thirteen virtues (135-37).

In the late Renaissance, Machiavelli contended that human beings were by nature "ungrateful" and "mutable" (1240), and Montaigne thought them "miserable and puny" (1343).

If a quotation comes at the end of the sentence, clause, or phrase, insert the parenthetical reference between the closing quotation mark and the concluding punctuation mark.

Ernst Rose submits, "The highly spiritual view of the world presented in Siddartha exercised its appeal on West and East alike" (74).

If the quotation, whether of poetry or prose, is set off from the text (see 2.6.2-3), skip two spaces after the concluding punctuation mark of the quotation and insert the parenthetical reference.

John K. Mahon offers this comment on the War of 1812:

> **Financing the war was very difficult at the time. Baring Brothers, a banking firm of the enemy country, handled routine accounts for the**

> United States overseas, but the firm would take on no loans. The loans were in the end absorbed by wealthy Americans at great hazard--also, as it turned out, at great profit to them. (385)

Elizabeth Bishop's "In the Waiting Room" is rich in evocative detail:

> It was winter. It got dark
> early. The waiting room
> was full of grown-up people,
> arctics and overcoats,
> lamps and magazines. (6-10)

If you need to document several sources for a statement, you may cite them in a note to avoid unduly disrupting the text (see 5.6). If you quote several times from the same page within a single paragraph—and no quotation from another source intervenes—you may give a single parenthetical reference after the last quotation.

5.5. Sample references

Each of the following sections concludes with a list of the works it cites. Note that the lists for the first five sections (5.5.1 to 5.5.5) do not include more than one work by the same author. On citing two or more works by an author, see 5.5.6.

5.5.1. Citing an entire work

If you wish to cite an entire work, rather than part of the work, it is usually preferable to include the author's name in the text rather than in a parenthetical reference.

But Dan W. Brock has offered another view.

Seller's <u>Ethnic Theater in the United States</u> includes many examples of this influence.

Kurosawa's <u>Rashomon</u> was one of the first Japanese films to attract a Western audience.

John Ciardi's remarks drew warm applause.

I vividly recall the Caldwell production of <u>La Traviata</u>.

Pattis's introduction to computer programming has received widespread praise.

Gilbert and Gubar broke new ground on the subject.

Edens et al. have a useful collection of essays on teaching Shakespeare.

Works Cited

Brock, Dan W. "The Value of Prolonging Life." <u>Philosophical Studies</u> 50 (1986): 401-26.

Caldwell, Sarah, dir. and cond. <u>La Traviata</u>. By Giuseppe Verdi. With Beverly Sills.

Opera Co. of Boston. Orpheum Theatre, Boston. 4 Nov. 1972.

Ciardi, John. Address. Opening General Sess. NCTE Convention, Washington. 19 Nov. 1982.

Edens, Walter, et al., eds. *Teaching Shakespeare*. Princeton: Princeton UP, 1977.

Gilbert, Sandra M., and Susan Gubar. *The Madwoman in the Attic: The Woman Writer and the Nineteenth-Century Literary Imagination*. New Haven: Yale UP, 1979.

Kurosawa, Akira, dir. *Rashomon*. With Toshiro Mifune and Michiko Kyo. Daiei, 1950.

Pattis, Richard E. *Karel the Robot: A Gentle Introduction to the Art of Programming*. Computer software. Cybertronics, 1981.

Seller, Maxine Schwartz, ed. *Ethnic Theater in the United States*. Westport: Greenwood, 1983.

5.5.2. Citing part of an article or of a book

If you quote, paraphrase, or otherwise use a specific passage in a book or article, give the relevant page numbers. When the author's name is in the text, give only the page reference in parentheses; but if the context does not clearly identify the author, add the author's last name before the page reference. Leave a space between them, but do not insert punctuation or write the word *page(s)* or the abbreviation *p.* or *pp.* If you have used only one volume of a multivolume work and have included the volume number in the bibliographic entry, you need give only page numbers in the reference (see Daiches example), but if you have used more than one volume of the work, you must cite both volume and page numbers (see 5.5.3).

Daiches is useful on the Restoration (538-89), as he is on other periods.

Kenneth Clark raised some interesting questions concerning artistic "masterpieces" (1-5, 12-13).

Another particularly appealing passage is the opening of García Márquez's story "A Very Old Man with Enormous Wings" (105).

Among intentional spoonerisms, the "punlike metathesis of distinctive features may serve to weld together words etymologically unrelated but close in their sound and meaning" (Jakobson and Waugh 304).

In Hansberry's play A Raisin in the Sun the rejection of Lindner's tempting offer permits Walter's family to pursue the new life they had long dreamed about (274-75).

As Katharina M. Wilson has written, "Intended or not, the echoes of Tertullian's exhortations in the Utopia provide yet another level of ambiguity to More's ironic commentary on social and moral conditions both in sixteenth-century Europe and in Nowhere-Land" (73).

A 1983 report found "a decline in the academic quality of students choosing teaching as a career" (Hook 10).

Works Cited

Clark, Kenneth. What Is a Masterpiece? London: Thames, 1979.

Daiches, David. A Critical History of English Literature. 2nd ed. Vol. 2. New York: Ronald, 1970.

García Márquez, Gabriel. "A Very Old Man with Enormous Wings." "Leaf Storm" and Other Stories. Trans. Gregory Rabassa. New York: Harper, 1972. 105-12.

Hansberry, Lorraine. A Raisin in the Sun. Black Theater: A Twentieth-Century Collection of the Work of Its Best Playwrights. Ed. Lindsay Patterson. New York: Dodd, 1971. 221-76.

Hook, Janet. "Raise Standards of Admission, Colleges Urged." Chronicle of Higher Education 4 May 1983: 1+.

Jakobson, Roman, and Linda R. Waugh. The Sound

Shape of Language. Bloomington: Indiana UP, 1979.

Wilson, Katharina M. "Tertullian's De cultu foeminarum and Utopia." Moreana 73 (1982): 69-74.

5.5.3. Citing volume and page numbers of a multivolume work

To cite a volume number as well as page numbers of a multivolume work, separate the two by a colon and a space: (Wellek 2: 1–10). Use neither the words *volume* and *page* nor their abbreviations. It is understood that the number before the colon identifies the volume and the number(s) after the colon the page(s). If, however, you wish to refer parenthetically to an entire volume of a multivolume work, so that there is no need to cite pages, place a comma after the author's name and include the abbreviation *vol.*: (Wellek, vol. 2). If you integrate such a reference into a sentence, spell out *volume* instead of abbreviating it: "In volume 2, Wellek deals with. . . ."

Daiches is as useful on the Restoration (2: 538-89) as he is on Anglo-Saxon literature (1: 3-30).

Interest in Afro-American literature in the 1960s and 1970s inevitably led to "a significant reassessment of the aesthetic and humanistic achievements of black writers" (Inge, Duke, and Bryer 1: v).

Between the years 1945 and 1972, the political

party system in the United States underwent profound changes (Schlesinger, vol. 4).

Works Cited

Daiches, David. A Critical History of English Literature. 2nd ed. 2 vols. New York: Ronald, 1970.

Inge, M. Thomas, Maurice Duke, and Jackson R. Bryer, eds. Black American Writers: Bibliographical Essays. 2 vols. New York: St. Martin's, 1978.

Schlesinger, Arthur M., gen. ed. History of U.S. Political Parties. 4 vols. New York: Chelsea, 1973.

5.5.4. Citing a work listed by title

In a parenthetical reference to a work alphabetized by title in the list of works cited, the title (if brief), or a shortened version, precedes the page number(s). Omit a page reference, however, if you are citing a one-page article or, of course, a nonprint source. When abbreviating the title of an anonymous work, begin with the word by which it is alphabetized in the list of works cited. It would be a mistake, for example, to shorten *Glossary of Terms Used in Heraldry* to *Heraldry*, since your reader would then look for the bibliographic entry under *H* rather than *G*. (For citing books by corporate authors, see 5.5.5.)

The nine grades of mandarins were "distinguished by the color of the button on the hats of office" ("Mandarin").

According to the Handbook of Korea, much Korean sculpture is associated with Buddhism (241-47).

Computerworld devoted a thoughtful editorial to the issue of government and technology ("Uneasy Silence"), and one hopes that such public discussion will continue in the future.

Later, when the characters are confronted by tragedy, they take on greater depth ("Joy Ride").

Works Cited

A Handbook of Korea. 4th ed. Seoul: Korean Overseas Information Service, Ministry of Culture and Information, 1982.

"The Joy Ride." Writ. Alfred Shaughnessy. Upstairs, Downstairs. Created by Eileen Atkins and Jean Marsh. Dir. Bill Bain. Prod. John Hawkesworth. Masterpiece Theatre. Introd. Alistair Cooke. PBS. WGBH, Boston. 6 Feb. 1977.

"Mandarin." Encyclopedia Americana. 1980 ed.

"An Uneasy Silence." Editorial. Computerworld 28 Mar. 1983: 54.

5.5.5. Citing a work by a corporate author

To cite a work listed by a corporate author, you may use the author's name followed by a page reference: (United Nations, Economic Commission for Africa 79–86). It is better, however, to include such a long name in the text to avoid interrupting the reading with an extended parenthetical reference.

In 1963 the United Nations' Economic Commission for Africa predicted that Africa would evolve into an industrially advanced economy within fifty years (1, 4-6).

The Commission on the Humanities has concluded that "the humanities are inescapably bound to literacy" (69).

Works Cited

Commission on the Humanities. The Humanities in American Life: Report of the Commission on the Humanities. Berkeley: U of California P, 1980.

United Nations. Economic Commission for Africa. Industrial Growth in Africa. New York: United Nations, 1963.

5.5.6. Citing two or more works by the same author(s)

To cite one of two or more works by the same author(s), put a comma after the last name(s) of the author(s) and add the title of the work (if brief), or a shortened version, and the relevant page reference: (Borroff, *Wallace Stevens* 2), (Durant and Durant, *Age of Voltaire* 214–48). If you state the author's name in the text, give only the title and page reference: (*Wallace Stevens* 2), (*Age of Voltaire* 214–48). If you include both the author's name and the title in the text, indicate only the pertinent page number(s) in parentheses: (2), (214–48).

Borroff finds Stevens "dominated by two powerful and contending temperamental strains" (Wallace Stevens 2).

In The Age of Voltaire the Durants portray eighteenth-century England as "a humble satellite" in the world of music and art (214-48).

According to E. L. Doctorow, "The Dreiserian universe is composed of merchants, workers, club-men, managers, actors, salesmen, doormen, cops, derelicts--a Balzacian population unified by the rules of commerce and the ideals of property and social position" (Introduction ix).

The Gawain Poet has been called a "master of juxtaposition" (Borroff, Sir Gawain viii) and has been praised for other poetic achievements.

To Will and Ariel Durant, creative men and women make "history forgivable by enriching our heritage and our lives" (Dual Autobiography 406).

The brief but dramatic conclusion of chapter 13 of Doctorow's <u>Welcome to Hard Times</u> constitutes the climax of the novel (209-12).

Works Cited

Borroff, Marie, trans. <u>Sir Gawain and the Green Knight</u>. New York: Norton, 1967.

---, ed. <u>Wallace Stevens: A Collection of Critical Essays</u>. Englewood Cliffs: Prentice, 1963.

Doctorow, E. L. Introduction. <u>Sister Carrie</u>. By Theodore Dreiser. New York: Bantam, 1982. v-xi.

---. <u>Welcome to Hard Times</u>. 1960. New York: Bantam, 1976.

Durant, Will, and Ariel Durant. <u>The Age of Voltaire</u>. New York: Simon, 1965. Vol. 9 of <u>The Story of Civilization</u>. 11 vols. 1935-75.

---. <u>A Dual Autobiography</u>. New York: Simon, 1977.

5.5.7. Citing indirect sources

Whenever you can, take material from the original source, not a secondhand one. Sometimes, however, only an indirect source is available—for example, someone's published account of another's spoken remarks. If you quote or paraphrase a quotation from another book, put the abbreviation *qtd. in* ("quoted in") before the indirect source you cite in your parenthetical reference. (You may document the original source in a note; see 5.6.1.)

Samuel Johnson admitted that Edmund Burke was an "extraordinary man" (qtd. in Boswell 2: 450).

The remarks of Bernardo Segni and Lionardo Salviati demonstrate that they were not faithful disciples of Aristotle (qtd. in Weinberg 1:405, 616-17).

Works Cited

Boswell, James. The Life of Johnson. Ed. George Birkbeck Hill and L. F. Powell. 6 vols. Oxford: Clarendon, 1934-50.

Weinberg, Bernard. A History of Literary Criticism in the Italian Renaissance. 2 vols. Chicago: U of Chicago P, 1961.

5.5.8. Citing literary works

In references to classic prose works available in several editions (e.g., novels and plays), it is helpful to provide more information than just the page number of the edition used; a chapter number, for example, would enable readers to locate a quotation in any copy of the novel. In such references, give the page number first, add a semicolon, and then give other identifying information, using appropriate abbreviations: (130; ch. 9), (271; bk. 4, ch. 2).

When we first encounter Raskolnikov in Crime and Punishment, Dostoevsky presents us with a man contemplating a terrible act but terrified of meeting his talkative landlady on the stairs (1; pt. 1, ch. 1).

Mary Wollstonecraft recollects in A Vindication of the Rights of Woman many "women who, not led by degrees to proper studies, and not permitted to choose for themselves, have indeed been overgrown children" (185; ch. 13, sec. 2).

In one version of the story, William Tell's son urges his reluctant father to shoot the arrow (Sastre 315; sc. 6).

In citing classic verse plays and poems, omit page numbers altogether and cite by division(s) (e.g., act, scene, canto, book, part) and line(s), with periods separating the various numbers—for example, *Iliad* 9.19 refers to book 9, line 19, of Homer's *Iliad.* If you are citing only line numbers, do not use the abbreviation *l.* or *ll.*, which can be confused with numerals. Instead, initially use the word *line* or *lines* and, once you have established that the numbers designate lines, use the numbers alone.

In general, use arabic numerals rather than roman numerals for division and page numbers. Although you must use roman numerals, of course, when citing pages of a preface or other section that are so numbered, designate volumes, parts, books, and chapters with arabic numerals even if your source does not. Some instructors prefer roman numerals, however, for citing acts and scenes in plays (*King Lear* IV.i), but if your instructor does not recommend this practice, use arabic numerals (*King Lear* 4.1). On numbers, see 2.4.

When included in parenthetical references, the titles of the books of the Bible and of famous literary works are often abbreviated (1 Chron. 21.8, Rev. 21.3, *Oth.* 4.2.7–13, *FQ* 3.3.53.3). The most widely used and accepted abbreviations for such titles are listed in 6.7. Follow prevailing practices, as indicated by your sources, for other abbreviations (*Troilus* for Chaucer's *Troilus and Criseyde*, *DQ* for Cervantes's *Don Quixote*, *PL* for Milton's *Paradise Lost*, "Nightingale" for Keats's "Ode to a Nightingale," etc.). In the following example the reference is to lines 1791 and 1792 of book 5 of Chaucer's *Troilus and Criseyde*.

Chaucer urges one of his "litel boks" to kiss "the steppes, where as thow seest pace / Virgile, Ovide, Omer, Lucan, and Stace" (Troilus 5.1791-92), using a figure much imitated by later English poets.

Works Cited

Chaucer, Geoffrey. The Works of Geoffrey Chaucer. Ed. F. N. Robinson. 2nd ed. Boston: Houghton, 1957.

Dostoevsky, Feodor. Crime and Punishment. Trans. Jessie Coulson. Ed. George Gibian. New York: Norton, 1964.

Sastre, Alfonso. Sad Are the Eyes of William Tell. Trans. Leonard Pronko. The New Wave Spanish Drama. Ed. George Wellwarth. New York: New York UP, 1970. 165-321.

Wollstonecraft, Mary. A Vindication of the Rights of Woman. Ed. Carol H. Poston. New York: Norton, 1975.

5.5.9. Citing more than one work in a single parenthetical reference

If you wish to include two or more works in a single parenthetical reference, cite each work as you normally would in a reference, but use semicolons to separate the citations.

(Frye 42; Brée 101-33)

(National Committee 25-35; Brody C5)

(Potter et al., vol. 1; Boyle 96-125)

(Wellek and Warren; Booth, Critical Understanding 45-52)

(Blocker, Plummer, and Richardson 52-57; Commission on the Humanities 15)

(Booth, "Kenneth Burke's" 22; Cassirer 1: 295-319)

Keep in mind, however, that long parenthetical references—for example, (Stratman; Potter et al. 1: 176-202; Bondanella and Bondanella, "Lauda"; Curley ii-vii; Rey-Flaud 37-43, 187-201; Pikeryng A2r)—may prove intrusive and disconcerting to the reader. To avoid an excessive disruption, cite multiple sources in a note rather than in parentheses in the text (see 5.6.2).

Works Cited

Blocker, Clyde E., Robert H. Plummer, and Richard C. Richardson, Jr. The Two-Year College: A Social Synthesis. Englewood Cliffs: Prentice, 1965.

Bondanella, Peter, and Julia Conaway Bondanella, eds. Dictionary of Italian Literature. Westport: Greenwood, 1979.

Booth, Wayne C. Critical Understanding: The Powers and Limits of Pluralism. Chicago: U of Chicago P, 1979.

---. "Kenneth Burke's Way of Knowing." Critical Inquiry 1 (1974): 1-22.

Boyle, Anthony T. "The Epistemological Evolution of Renaissance Utopian Literature: 1516-1657." Diss. New York U, 1983.

Brée, Germaine. Women Writers in France: Variations on a Theme. New Brunswick: Rutgers UP, 1973.

Brody, Jane. "Heart Attacks: Turmoil beneath the Calm." New York Times 21 June 1983, late ed.: C1+.

Cassirer, Ernst. The Philosophy of Symbolic Forms. Trans. Ralph Manheim. 3 vols. New Haven: Yale UP, 1955.

Commission on the Humanities. The Humanities in American Life: Report of the Commission on the Humanities. Berkeley: U of California P, 1980.

Curley, Michael, trans. Physiologus. Austin: U of Texas P, 1979.

Frye, Northrop. Anatomy of Criticism: Four Essays. Princeton: Princeton UP, 1957.

National Committee on Careers for Older Americans. Older Americans: An Untapped Resource. Washington: Acad. for Educ. Dev., 1979.

Pikeryng, John. A Newe Enterlude of Vice Conteyninge the Historye of Horestes. London, 1567.

Potter, G. R., et al. The New Cambridge Modern History. 14 vols. Cambridge: Cambridge UP, 1957-70.

Rey-Flaud, Henri. Pour une dramaturgie du Moyen Age. Paris: PUF, 1980.

Stratman, Carl J., comp. and ed. Bibliography of English Printed Tragedy, 1565-1900. Carbondale: Southern Illinois UP, 1966.

Wellek, René, and Austin Warren. Theory of Literature. 3rd ed. New York: Harcourt, 1962.

5.6. Using notes with parenthetical documentation

Two kinds of notes may be used with parenthetical documentation:

1. Content notes offering the reader comment, explanation, or information that the text cannot accommodate
2. Bibliographic notes containing either several sources or evaluative comments on sources

In providing this sort of supplementary information, place a superscript arabic numeral at the appropriate place in the text (see 5.8.2) and write the note after a matching numeral either at the end of the text (an endnote) or at the bottom of the page (a footnote) (see 5.8.4).

5.6.1. Content notes

Avoid essaylike notes, which divert the reader's attention from the primary text. In general, if you cannot fit comments into the text, omit them unless they are essential to justify or clarify what you have written. You may use a note, for example, to give full publication facts for an original source for which you cite an indirect source and perhaps to explain why you worked from secondary material.

The remarks of Bernardo Segni and Lionardo Salviati demonstrate that they were not faithful disciples of Aristotle.[1]

Note

[1] Bernardo Segni, Rettorica et poetica d'Aristotile (Florence, 1549) 281, qtd. in Weinberg 1: 405; Lionardo Salviati, Poetica d'Aristotile parafrasata e comentata (Florence, 1586) ms. 2.2.11, Bibl. Naz. Centrale, Florence, 140v, qtd. in Weinberg 1: 616-17.

For more information on using notes for documentation purposes, see 5.8.

Work Cited

Weinberg, Bernard. A History of Literary Criticism in the Italian Renaissance. 2 vols. Chicago: U of Chicago P, 1961.

5.6.2. Bibliographic notes

Use notes for evaluative comments on sources and for references containing numerous citations.

For older people, the past decade has represented the best of times and the worst of times.[1]

It is a difficult task to attempt to chart the development of drama in the context of medieval and Renaissance Europe.[2]

Notes

[1] For contrasting points of view, see National Committee and Brody C5.

[2] For a sampling of useful source materials, see Potter et al. 1: 176-202; Bondanella and Bondanella, "Lauda"; Rey-Flaud 37-43, 187-201; and Stratman.

Works Cited

Bondanella, Peter, and Julia Conaway Bondanella, eds. Dictionary of Italian Literature. Westport: Greenwood, 1979.

Brody, Jane. "Heart Attacks: Turmoil beneath the Calm." New York Times 21 June 1983, late ed.: C1+.

National Committee on Careers for Older Americans. Older Americans: An Untapped Resource. Washington: Acad. for Educ. Dev., 1979.

Potter, G. R., et al. The New Cambridge Modern History. 14 vols. Cambridge: Cambridge UP, 1957-70.

Rey-Flaud, Henri. Pour une dramaturgie du Moyen Age. Paris: PUF, 1980.

Stratman, Carl J., comp. and ed. Bibliography of English Printed Tragedy, 1565-1900. Carbondale: Southern Illinois UP, 1966.

5.7. Other types of parenthetical documentation

Other types of parenthetical documentation include (1) the author-date system, (2) the number system, and (3) the placement of full publication information in the text.

5.7.1. Author-date system

The author-date system, the most common in the social and physical sciences, requires that a parenthetical reference include the author's last name and the work's year of publication (unless given in the text), followed by a comma and the page reference: (Wilson 1982, 73). Information cited in the text is omitted from the parenthetical reference.

This system also requires a slight change in bibliographic form: the year of publication immediately follows the author's name, so that the reader can quickly find the appropriate entry. The title of the work and the remaining publication information complete the citation. If the list includes more than one work by an author, the entries are arranged chronologically. If two or more works by the same author were published in a given year, each is assigned a lowercase letter (1979a, 1979b).

In The Age of Voltaire the Durants portray eighteenth-century England as a "humble satellite" in the world of music and art (1965, 214-48).

The alazon is a "self-deceiving or self-deceived character in fiction" (Frye 1957a, 365).

Daiches is useful on the Restoration (1970, 2: 538-89), as he is on other periods.

As Katharina M. Wilson has written, "Intended or not, the echoes of Tertullian's exhortations in the Utopia provide yet another level of ambiguity to More's ironic commentary on social and moral conditions both in sixteenth-century Europe and in Nowhere-Land" (1982, 73).

There are several excellent essays in the volume Sound and Poetry (Frye 1957b).

To Will and Ariel Durant, creative men and women make "history forgivable by enriching our heritage and our lives" (1977, 406).

Works Cited

Daiches, David. 1970. A Critical History of English Literature. 2nd ed. 2 vols. New York: Ronald.

Durant, Will, and Ariel Durant. 1965. The Age of Voltaire. New York: Simon. Vol. 9 of The Story of Civilization. 11 vols. 1935-75.

---. 1977. A Dual Autobiography. New York: Simon.

Frye, Northrop. 1957a. Anatomy of Criticism: Four Essays. Princeton: Princeton UP.

---, ed. 1957b. Sound and Poetry. New York: Columbia UP.

Wilson, Katharina M. 1982. "Tertullian's De cultu foeminarum and Utopia." Moreana 73: 69-74.

5.7.2. Number system

In the number system, arabic numerals designate entries in the list of works cited and appear (sometimes underlined) in parenthetical documentation followed by commas and the relevant page references. With this system, the year of publication remains at the end of the bibliographic entry, and the works may be listed in any useful order. (In the sciences, for example, they are frequently arranged in the order in which they are first cited in the text.)

The alazon is a "self-deceiving or self-deceived character in fiction" (2, 365).

In The Age of Voltaire the Durants portray eighteenth-century England as a "humble satellite" in the world of music and art (1, 214-48).

There are several excellent essays in the volume Sound and Poetry (3).

Works Cited

1. Durant, Will, and Ariel Durant. The Age of Voltaire. New York: Simon, 1965. Vol. 9 of The Story of Civilization. 11 vols. 1935-75.

2. Frye, Northrop. Anatomy of Criticism: Four Essays. Princeton: Princeton UP, 1957.

3. ---, ed. Sound and Poetry. New York: Columbia UP, 1957.

5.7.3. Complete citations in the text

The practice of placing full publication information in parenthetical references is seldom followed because it deprives the reader of the benefits of a list of works cited and interrupts the flow of the text. Sometimes, however, it is adopted in bibliographic studies or in works requiring few references. As in other systems, information given in the text is not repeated in the reference. Commas replace separating periods, and square brackets are used for parentheses within parentheses.

The alazon, as Northrop Frye describes it, is a "self-deceiving or self-deceived character in fiction" (<u>Anatomy of Criticism: Four Essays</u>, Princeton: Princeton UP, 1957, 365).

In his <u>A Critical History of English Literature</u> David Daiches is useful on the Restoration (2nd ed., vol. 2, New York: Ronald, 1970, 538-89), as he is on other periods.

5.8. Using notes for documentation

Another system of documentation entails using endnotes or footnotes to cite sources.

5.8.1. Documentation notes versus the list of works cited and parenthetical references

If you use notes for documentation, you may not need a list of works cited or a bibliography. (Check your instructor's preference.) The first note referring to a source includes the publication information found in a bibliographic entry—the author's name, the title, and the publication facts—as well as the specific page reference. (Subsequent references to a work require less information; see 5.8.8.) Note form, however, differs slightly from bibliographic form (see 5.8.3), and note numbers replace parenthetical references at appropriate points in the text to draw the reader's attention to citations (see 5.8.2). Documentation notes appear either at the end of the text, as endnotes, or at the bottoms of relevant pages, as footnotes (see 5.8.4).

5.8.2. Note numbers

Number notes consecutively, starting from 1, throughout a research paper, except for any notes accompanying special material, such as a figure or a table (see 3.7). Do not number them by page or designate them by asterisks or other symbols. Type note numbers as "superior," or "superscript," arabic numerals (i.e., raised slightly above the line), without periods, parentheses, or slashes. The numbers follow punctuation marks, except dashes. In general, to avoid interrupting the continuity of the text, place a note number, like a parenthetical reference, at the end of the sentence, clause, or phrase containing the material quoted or referred to.

5.8.3. Note form versus bibliographic form

With some exceptions, documentary notes and bibliographic entries provide the same information but differ in form.

Bibliographic form

A bibliographic entry has three main divisions, each followed by a period: the author's name reversed for alphabetizing, the title, and the publishing data.

Frye, Northrop. Anatomy of Criticism: Four Essays. Princeton: Princeton UP, 1957.

Note form

A documentary note has four main divisions, with a period only at the end: the author's name in normal order, followed by a comma; the title; the publishing data in parentheses; and a page reference.

[1] Northrop Frye, Anatomy of Criticism: Four Essays (Princeton: Princeton UP, 1957) 52.

5.8.4. Endnotes and footnotes

In research papers, make all notes endnotes, unless you are instructed otherwise. As their name implies, endnotes appear after the text, starting on a new page numbered in sequence with the preceding page. Center the title *Notes* one inch from the top, double-space, indent five spaces from the left margin, and type the note number, without punctuation, slightly above the line. Leave a space and type the reference. If the note extends to two or more lines, begin subsequent lines at the left margin. Type the notes consecutively, double-spaced, and number all pages.

Footnotes appear at the bottoms of pages, beginning four lines (two double spaces) below the text. Single-space footnotes but double-space between them. When a note continues on the following page, type a solid line across the new page one line (one double space) below the last line of the text and continue the note four lines (a total of two double spaces) below the text. Footnotes for the new page immediately follow the note continued from the previous page.

5.8.5. Sample first note references: Books

Bibliographic entries corresponding to the following sample notes appear in the sections indicated in parentheses after the headings. Consult the appropriate section if you need additional information on citing a particular type of reference.

a. A book by a single author (4.5.1)

[1] Carol Fairbanks, Prairie Women: Images in American and Canadian Fiction (New Haven: Yale UP, 1986) 32.

b. An anthology or compilation (4.5.2)

[2] Fred J. Nichols, ed. and trans., An Anthology of Neo-Latin Poetry (New Haven: Yale UP, 1979) vii-viii.

c. A book by multiple authors (4.5.4)

[3] Jason Berry, Jonathan Foose, and Tad Jones, Up from the Cradle: New Orleans Music since World War II (Athens: U of Georgia P, 1986) 52-57.

d. A book by a corporate author (4.5.6)

[4] Commission on the Humanities, The Humanities in American Life: Report of the Commission on the Humanities (Berkeley: U of California P, 1980) 69.

e. An anonymous book (4.5.7)

[5] A Guide to Our Federal Lands (Washington: Natl. Geographic Soc., 1984) 241-47.

f. A work in an anthology (4.5.8)

[6] Naomi Lazard, "In Answer to Your Query," The Norton Book of Light Verse, ed. Russell Baker (New York: Norton, 1986) 52.

[7] Lorraine Hansberry, A Raisin in the Sun, Black Theater: A Twentieth-Century Collection of the Work of Its Best Playwrights, ed. Lindsay Patterson (New York: Dodd, 1971) 265-66.

g. An introduction, preface, foreword, or afterword (4.5.9)

[8] Edgar Johnson, afterword, David Copperfield, by Charles Dickens (New York: Signet-NAL, 1962) 875.

h. A multivolume work (4.5.11)

[9] David Daiches, A Critical History of English Literature, 2nd ed., vol. 2 (New York: Ronald, 1970) 538-39.

[10] Arthur M. Schlesinger, gen. ed., History of U.S. Political Parties, vol. 4 (New York: Chelsea, 1973).

i. An "edition" (4.5.12)

[11] Geoffrey Chaucer, The Works of Geoffrey Chaucer, ed. F. N. Robinson, 2nd ed. (Boston: Houghton, 1957) 545.

[12] Jo Ann Boydston, ed., Psychology, by John Dewey (Carbondale: Southern Illinois UP, 1967) 85-87, vol. 2 of The Early Works, 1882-1898.

j. A translation (4.5.13)

[13] Johann Wolfgang von Goethe, Faust, trans. Walter Arndt, ed. Cyrus Hamlin (New

York: Norton, 1976) 157.

[14] Patrick Creagh, trans., The Uses of Literature, by Italo Calvino (San Diego: Harcourt, 1986) 1-5.

k. A republished book (4.5.14)

[15] Alice Walker, The Color Purple (1982; New York: Pocket, 1985) 209-12.

l. An article in a reference book (4.5.15)

[16] "Melodeon," Encyclopedia Americana, 1985 ed.

m. A pamphlet (4.5.16)

[17] Career as an Aerospace-Aircraft Engineer (Chicago: Inst. for Research, 1978) 11-16.

n. Government publications (4.5.17)

[18] United Nations, Economic Commission for Africa, Industrial Growth in Africa (New York: United Nations, 1963) 4-6.

o. A book in a series (4.5.18)

[19] Joan Hinde Stewart, Colette, Twayne's World Authors Ser. 679 (Boston: Twayne, 1983) 62.

p. A publisher's imprint (4.5.19)

[20] Jonathan Kozol, Illiterate America (New York: Anchor-Doubleday, 1985) 206.

q. Multiple publishers (4.5.20)

[21] J. Wight Duff, A Literary History of Rome: From the Origins to the Close of the Golden Age, ed. A. M. Duff, 3rd ed. (1953; London: Benn; New York: Barnes, 1967) 88.

r. Published proceedings of a conference (4.5.21)

[22] Alan M. Gordon and Evelyn Rugg, eds., Actas del Sexto Congreso Internacional de Hispanistas celebrado en Toronto del 22 al 26 agosto 1977 (Toronto: Dept. of Spanish and Portuguese, U of Toronto, 1980) v-vii.

s. A book in a language other than English (4.5.22)

[23] Barbara Wachowicz, Marie jehoživota (Praha [Prague]: Lidové, 1979) 1-5.

t. A book with a title within its title (4.5.23)

[24] Leonard Mades, The Armor and the Brocade: A Study of Don Quijote and The Courtier (New York: Americas, 1968) 5-11.

u. A book published before 1900 (4.5.24)

[25] John Dewey, The Study of Ethics: A Syllabus (Ann Arbor, 1894) 104.

v. A book without stated publication information or pagination (4.5.25)

[26] Zvi Malachi, ed., Proceedings of the International Conference on Literary and Linguistic Computing ([Tel Aviv]: [Fac. of Humanities, Tel Aviv U], n.d.) 1-3.

w. An unpublished dissertation (4.5.26)

[27] Nancy Kay Johnson, "Cultural and Psychosocial Determinants of Health and Illness," diss., U of Washington, 1980, 34.

x. A published dissertation (4.5.27)

[28] Rudolf E. Dietze, Ralph Ellison: The Genesis of an Artist, diss., U Erlangen-Nürnberg, 1982, Erlanger Beiträge zur Sprach- und Kunstwissenschaft 70 (Nürnberg: Carl, 1982) 168.

5.8.6. Sample first note references: Articles in periodicals

For additional information on citing the following types of sources, consult the related sections for bibliographic entries, indicated in parentheses after the headings.

a. An article from a newspaper (4.7.1)

[1] Jonathan Fuerbringer, "Budgetary Rhythms," New York Times 20 Mar. 1987, late ed.: A8.

[2] David Wheeler, "Artificial-Intelligence Researchers Develop Electronic 'Tutors' to Aid Learning Process," Chronicle of Higher Education 20 May 1987: 6.

b. An article from a magazine (4.7.2)

[3] Douglas H. Lamb and Glenn D. Reeder, "Reliving Golden Days," Psychology Today June 1986: 22.

c. An article in a scholarly journal with continuous pagination (4.7.3)

[4] Zita Réger, "The Functions of Imitation in Child Language," Applied Psycholinguistics 7 (1986): 352.

d. An article in a scholarly journal that pages each issue separately (4.7.4)

[5] Frederick Barthelme, "Architecture," Kansas Quarterly 13.3-4 (1981): 77-78.

e. An article in a scholarly journal that uses only issue numbers (4.7.5)

[6] Angele Botros Samaan, "Death and the Death Penalty in More's Utopia and Some Other Utopian Novels," Moreana 90 (1986): 10-11.

f. An article from a journal with more than one series (4.7.6)

[7] William H. Gass, "Some Snapshots from the Soviet Zone," Kenyon Review ns 8.4 (1986): 43.

[8] Harvey H. Jackson, "Hugh Bryan and the Evangelical Movement in Colonial South Carolina," William and Mary Quarterly 3rd ser. 43 (1986): 600-02.

g. An editorial (4.7.7)

[9] "A Fee, Not a Ban, on Auto Progress," editorial, New York Times 24 May 1987, late ed., sec. 4: 16.

h. An anonymous article (4.7.8)

10 "Drunkproofing Automobiles," Time 6 Apr. 1987: 37.

i. A letter to the editor (4.7.9)

11 Harry Levin, letter, Partisan Review 47 (1980): 320.

j. A review (4.7.10)

12 Lucia K. B. Hall, rev. of God and the New Physics, by Paul Davies, Humanist Nov.-Dec. 1986: 39.

13 Robert Craft, "The Maestro on the Market," rev. of Understanding Toscanini: How He Became an American Culture-God and Helped Create a New Audience for Old Music, by Joseph Horowitz, New York Review of Books 9 Apr. 1987: 20-22.

14 "The Cooling of an Admiration," rev. of Joyce, with Pound's Essays on Joyce, ed. Forrest Read, Times Literary Supplement 6 Mar. 1969: 239-40.

15 Rev. of Anthology of Danish Literature, ed. F. J. Billeskov Jansen and P. M. Mitchell, Times Literary Supplement 7 July 1972: 785.

k. An article whose title contains a quotation or a title within quotation marks (4.7.11)

16 E. E. Duncan-Jones, "Moore's 'A Kiss à l'Antique' and Keats's 'Ode on a Grecian Urn,'" Notes and Queries ns 28 (1981): 316-17.

l. An abstract from *Dissertation Abstracts* or *Dissertation Abstracts International* (4.7.12)

17 Nancy Kay Johnson, "Cultural and Psychosocial Determinants of Health and Illness," DAI 40 (1980): 4235B (U of Washington).

m. A serialized article (4.7.13)

18 Harrison T. Meserole and James M. Rambeau, "Articles on American Literature Appearing in Current Periodicals," American Literature 52 (1981): 688-90; 53 (1981): 164-66, 348-52.

19 Martin Gottlieb, "Times Square Development Plan: A Lesson in Politics and Power," New York Times 9 Mar. 1984, late ed.: B1; "Pressure and Compromise Saved Times Square Project," New York Times 10 Mar. 1984, late ed.: 25.

5.8.7. Sample first note references: Other sources

For additional information on the following types of documentation, consult the related sections for bibliographic entries, indicated in parentheses after the headings.

a. Computer software (4.8.1)

1 Connections, computer software, Krell Software, 1982.

2 Richard E. Pattis, Karel the Robot: A Gentle Introduction to the Art of Programming, computer software, Cybertronics, 1981.

b. Material from a computer service (4.8.2)

3 Howard Schomer, "South Africa: Beyond Fair Employment," Harvard Business Review May-June 1983: 145+ (Dialog file 122, item 119425 833160).

4 "Barbara Bush Turner," American Men and Women of Science, 15th ed. (Bowker, 1983) (Dialog file 236, item 0107406).

c. Material from an information service (4.8.3)

5 Bernard Spolsky, Navajo Language Maintenance: Six-Year-Olds in 1969, Navajo Reading Study Prog. Rept. 5 (Albuquerque: U of

New Mexico, 1969) 22 (ERIC ED 043 044).

6 Paul R. Streiff, Some Criteria for Designing Evaluation of TESOL Programs (ERIC, 1970) 10 (ED 040 385).

d. Television and radio programs (4.8.4)

7 "Agnes, the Indomitable de Mille," narr. Agnes de Mille, prod. Judy Kinberg, dir. Merrill Brockway, Dance in America, exec. prod. Jac Venza, Great Performances, PBS, WGBH, Boston, 8 May 1987.

e. Recordings (4.8.5)

8 Wolfgang A. Mozart, Symphony no. 35 in D and Overtures to The Marriage of Figaro, The Magic Flute, and Don Giovanni, cond. Antonia Brico, Mostly Mozart Orch., Columbia, M33888, 1979.

9 Robert Frost, "The Road Not Taken," Robert Frost Reads His Poetry, Caedmon, TC 1060, 1956.

10 D. K. Wilgus, Southern Folk Tales, audiotape, rec. 23-25 Mar. 1965, U of California, Los Angeles, Archives of Folklore, B.76.82 (7 ips, 7" reel).

11 David Lewiston, jacket notes, The

Balinese Gamelan: Music from the Morning of the World, Nonesuch Explorer Ser., H-2015, n.d.

f. Films, filmstrips, slide programs, and videotapes (4.8.6)

[12] It's a Wonderful Life, dir. Frank Capra, with James Stewart, Donna Reed, Lionel Barrymore, and Thomas Mitchell, RKO, 1946.

[13] Survey of the Animal Kingdom: The Invertebrates, sound filmstrip, by J. L. Wassink and C. R. Belinsky, Educational Images, 1985 (4 filmstrips, 4 audiocassettes).

g. Performances (4.8.7)

[14] Mikhail Baryshnikov, chor., Don Quixote, with Martine van Hamel and Kevin McKenzie, American Ballet Theater, Metropolitan Opera House, New York, 26 May 1986.

[15] Scott Joplin, Treemonisha, dir. Frank Corsaro, cond. Gunther Schuller, with Carmen Balthrop, Betty Allen, and Curtis Rayam, Houston Grand Opera, Miller Theatre, Boston, 18 May 1975.

h. Musical compositions (4.8.8)

[16] Ludwig van Beethoven, Symphony no. 7 in A, op. 92.

i. Works of art (4.8.9)

17 Rembrandt van Rijn, _Aristotle Contemplating the Bust of Homer_, Metropolitan Museum of Art, New York.

18 Mary Cassatt, _Mother and Child_, Wichita Art Museum, Wichita, slide 22 of _American Painting: 1560-1913_, by John Pearce (New York: McGraw, 1964).

j. Letters (4.8.10)

19 William Makepeace Thackeray, "To George Henry Lewes," 6 Mar. 1848, letter 452 of _Letters and Private Papers of William Makepeace Thackeray_, ed. Gordon N. Ray, vol. 2 (Cambridge: Harvard UP, 1946) 353-54.

20 Thomas Hart Benton, letter to John Charles Fremont, 22 June 1847, John Charles Fremont Papers, Southwest Museum Library, Los Angeles.

21 Aaron Copland, letter to the author, 17 May 1982.

k. Interviews (4.8.11)

22 Federico Fellini, "The Long Interview," _Juliet of the Spirits_, ed. Tullio Kezich, trans. Howard Greenfield (New York: Ballantine, 1966) 56.

23 Toni Morrison, interview, All Things Considered, National Public Radio, WNYC, New York, 16 Feb. 1986.

24 I. M. Pei, personal interview, 27 July 1983.

l. Maps and charts (4.8.12)

25 Canada, map (Chicago: Rand, 1987).

26 Grammar and Punctuation, chart (Grand Haven: School Zone, 1980).

m. Cartoons (4.8.13)

27 Garry Trudeau, "Doonesbury," cartoon, Star-Ledger [Newark, NJ] 27 May 1987: 25.

28 George Booth, cartoon, New Yorker 13 Apr. 1987: 25.

n. Lectures, speeches, and addresses (4.8.14)

29 Julia Kristeva, "Healing and Truth in Psychoanalysis," Div. on Psychological Approaches to Literature, MLA Convention, New York, 29 Dec. 1986.

30 John Ciardi, address, Opening General Sess., NCTE Convention, Washington, 19 Nov. 1982.

o. **Manuscripts and typescripts (4.8.15)**

[31] Mark Twain, Notebook 32, ts., Mark Twain Papers, U of California, Berkeley, 50.

p. **Legal references (4.8.16)**

[32] Stevens v. National Broadcasting Co., 148 USPQ 755 (CA Super. Ct. 1966).

5.8.8. Subsequent references

After fully documenting a work, use a shortened form in subsequent notes. As in parenthetical references (see 5.3), include enough information to identify the work. The author's last name alone, followed by the relevant page numbers, is usually adequate.

[4] Frye 345-47.

If you cite two or more works by the same author—for example, Northrop Frye's *Anatomy of Criticism* and his *Critical Path*—include a shortened form of the title following the author's last name in references after the first.

[8] Frye, Anatomy 278.

[9] Frye, Critical 1-3.

Repeat the information even when two references in sequence refer to the same work. The abbreviations *ibid.* and *op. cit.* are no longer recommended.

5.9. Other style manuals

Every scholarly field has its preferred format or "style." MLA style, as presented in this manual, is widely accepted in humanities disciplines. The following manuals describe the styles of other disciplines:

Biology

Council of Biology Editors. Style Manual Committee. *CBE Style Manual: A Guide for Authors, Editors, and Publishers in the Biological Sciences*. 5th ed. Bethesda: Council of Biology Editors, 1983.

Chemistry

American Chemical Society. *Handbook for Authors of Papers in American Chemical Society Publications*. Washington: American Chemical Soc., 1978.

Geology

United States. Geological Survey. *Suggestions to Authors of the Reports of the United States Geological Survey*. 6th ed. Washington: GPO, 1978.

Linguistics

Linguistic Society of America. *LSA Bulletin*, Dec. issue, annually.

Mathematics

American Mathematical Society. *A Manual for Authors of Mathematical Papers*. 7th ed. Providence: American Mathematical Soc., 1980.

Medicine

International Steering Committee of Medical Editors. "Uniform Requirements for Manuscripts Submitted to Biomedical Journals." *Annals of Internal Medicine* 90 (Jan. 1979): 95–99.

Physics

American Institute of Physics. Publications Board. *Style Manual for Guidance in the Preparation of Papers*. 3rd ed. New York: American Inst. of Physics, 1978.

Psychology

American Psychological Association. *Publication Manual of the American Psychological Association*. 3rd ed. Washington: American Psychological Assn., 1983.

Other available style manuals are addressed primarily to editors and concern procedures for converting a manuscript into type:

The Chicago Manual of Style. 13th ed. Chicago: U of Chicago P, 1982.
United States. Government Printing Office. *Style Manual*. Rev. ed. Washington: GPO, 1984.
Words into Type. By Marjorie E. Skillin, Robert M. Gay, et al. 3rd ed. Englewood Cliffs: Prentice, 1974.

For other style manuals and authors' guides, see John Bruce Howell, *Style Manuals of the English-Speaking World* (Phoenix: Oryx, 1983).

6. ABBREVIATIONS AND REFERENCE WORDS

6.1. Introduction

Abbreviations are commonly used in the list of works cited and in tabular material but rarely in the text of a research paper (except within parentheses). In choosing abbreviations, keep your audience in mind. While economy of space is important, clarity is more so. Spell out a term if the abbreviation may puzzle your readers.

When abbreviating, always use commonly accepted forms. In appropriate contexts, you may abbreviate days, months, and other measurements of time (see 6.2); states and countries (see 6.3); terms and reference words common in scholarship (see 6.4); and publishers' names (see 6.5).

The trend in abbreviation is to use neither periods after letters nor spaces between letters, especially for abbreviations made up of all capital letters.

BC NJ PhD S US

The chief exception to this trend continues to be the initials used for personal names: a period and a space ordinarily follow each initial.

H. L. Mencken

Likewise, most abbreviations that end in lowercase letters are followed by periods.

assn. Eng. fig.

introd. Mex. prod.

Whenever such an abbreviation is part of a longer one, the other parts also take periods and spaces.

H. Doc. n. pag. U. S. Dept. of Labor

In most abbreviations made up of lowercase letters that each represent a word, a period follows each letter, but no space intervenes between letters.

a.m. e.g. i.e. n.p.

But there are numerous exceptions.

ips ns os rpm

6.2. Time

Spell out the names of months in the text but abbreviate them in the list of works cited, except for May, June, and July. Whereas words denoting units of time are also spelled out in the text (seconds, minutes, weeks, months, years, centuries), some time designations are used *only* in abbreviated form (a.m., p.m., AD, BC, BCE, CE).

AD	*anno Domini* 'in the year of the Lord' (used before numerals: AD 14)
a.m.	*ante meridiem* 'before noon'
Apr.	April
Aug.	August
BC	before Christ (used after numerals: 19 BC)
BCE	before the Common Era
CE	Common Era
cent., cents.	century, centuries
Dec.	December
Feb.	February
Fri.	Friday
hr., hrs.	hour, hours
Jan.	January
Mar.	March
min., mins.	minute, minutes
mo., mos.	month, months
Mon.	Monday
Nov.	November
Oct.	October
p.m.	*post meridiem* 'after noon'
Sat.	Saturday
sec., secs.	second, seconds
Sep., Sept.	September
Sun.	Sunday
Thurs.	Thursday
Tues.	Tuesday
Wed.	Wednesday
wk., wks.	week, weeks
yr., yrs.	year, years

6.3. Geographical names

Spell out the names of states, territories, and possessions of the United States in the text, except, usually, in addresses and sometimes in parentheses. Likewise, spell out in the text the names of countries, with a few exceptions (e.g., USSR, BRD, DDR). In documentation, however, abbreviate the names of states, provinces, and countries.

AB	Alberta
Afr.	Africa
AK	Alaska
AL	Alabama
Alb.	Albania
AR	Arkansas
Arg.	Argentina
Arm.	Armenia
AS	American Samoa
Aus.	Austria
Austral.	Australia
AZ	Arizona
BC	British Columbia
Belg.	Belgium
Braz.	Brazil
BRD	Bundesrepublik Deutschland (see also W. Ger.)
Bulg.	Bulgaria
CA	California
Can.	Canada
CO	Colorado
CT	Connecticut
CZ	Canal Zone
Czech.	Czechoslovakia
DC	District of Columbia
DDR	Deutsche Demokratische Republik (see also E. Ger.)
DE	Delaware
Den.	Denmark
Ecua.	Ecuador
E. Ger.	East Germany (see also DDR)

Eng.	England
FL	Florida
Fr.	France
GA	Georgia
Gr.	Greece
Gt. Brit.	Great Britain
GU	Guam
HI	Hawaii
Hung.	Hungary
IA	Iowa
ID	Idaho
IL	Illinois
IN	Indiana
Ire.	Ireland
Isr.	Israel
It.	Italy
Jap.	Japan
KS	Kansas
KY	Kentucky
LA	Louisiana
LB	Labrador
Leb.	Lebanon
MA	Massachusetts
MB	Manitoba
MD	Maryland
ME	Maine
Mex.	Mexico
MI	Michigan
MN	Minnesota
MO	Missouri
MS	Mississippi
MT	Montana
NB	New Brunswick
NC	North Carolina
ND	North Dakota
NE	Nebraska
Neth.	Netherlands
NF	Newfoundland
NH	New Hampshire
NJ	New Jersey
NM	New Mexico
Norw.	Norway

NS	Nova Scotia
NT	Northwest Territories
NV	Nevada
NY	New York
NZ	New Zealand
OH	Ohio
OK	Oklahoma
ON	Ontario
OR	Oregon
PA	Pennsylvania
Pan.	Panama
PE	Prince Edward Island
Pol.	Poland
Port.	Portugal
PQ	Québec (Province du Québec)
PR	Puerto Rico
PRC	People's Republic of China
RI	Rhode Island
SC	South Carolina
Scot.	Scotland
SD	South Dakota
SK	Saskatchewan
Sp.	Spain
Swed.	Sweden
Switz.	Switzerland
TN	Tennessee
Turk.	Turkey
TX	Texas
UK	United Kingdom
US, USA	United States, United States of America
USSR	Union of Soviet Socialist Republics
UT	Utah
VA	Virginia
VI	Virgin Islands
VT	Vermont
WA	Washington
W. Ger.	West Germany (see also BRD)
WI	Wisconsin
WV	West Virginia
WY	Wyoming
YT	Yukon Territory
Yug.	Yugoslavia

6.4. Common scholarly abbreviations and reference words

The following list includes both abbreviations and reference words commonly used in humanities research studies in English. Abbreviations within parentheses are alternative, but not preferred, forms. Most of the abbreviations listed would replace the spelled forms only in parentheses, tabular material, or documentation.

abbr.	abbreviation, abbreviated
abr.	abridged, abridgment
acad.	academy
adapt.	adapted by, adaptation
adj.	adjective
adv.	adverb
app.	appendix
arch.	archaic
art.	article
assn.	association
assoc.	associate, associated
attrib.	attributed to
aux.	auxiliary
b.	born
BA	Bachelor of Arts
bib.	biblical
bibliog.	bibliography, bibliographer, bibliographic
biog.	biography, biographer, biographical
bk.	book
BM	British Museum, London (now British Library)
BS	Bachelor of Science
bull.	bulletin
©	copyright (© 1984)
c. (ca.)	*circa* 'about' (used with approximate dates: c. 1796)
cf.	*confer* 'compare' (*not* 'see')
ch., chs. (chap., chaps.)	chapter, chapters
chor.	choreographed by, choreographer
col.	column
coll.	college
colloq.	colloquial

comp.	compiled by, compiler
cond.	conducted by, conductor
Cong.	Congress
Cong. Rec.	*Congressional Record*
conj.	conjunction
Const.	Constitution
cont.	contents; continued
(contd.)	continued
d.	died
DA	Doctor of Arts
DA, *DAI*	*Dissertation Abstracts*, *Dissertation Abstracts International*
DAB	*Dictionary of American Biography*
dept.	department
dev.	developed by, development
dir.	directed by, director
diss.	dissertation
dist.	district
distr.	distributed by, distributor
div.	division
DNB	*Dictionary of National Biography*
doc.	document
ed.	edited by, editor, edition
EdD	Doctor of Education
eds.	editors, editions
educ.	education, educational
e.g.	*exempli gratia* 'for example' (rarely capitalized; set off by commas, unless preceded by a different punctuation mark)
enl.	enlarged (as in "rev. and enl. ed.")
esp.	especially
et al.	*et alii*, *et aliae* 'and others'
etc.	*et cetera* 'and so forth' (like most abbreviations, not appropriate in text)
ex.	example
fac.	faculty
fig.	figure
fl.	*floruit* 'flourished, reached greatest development or influence' (used before dates of historical figures when birth and death dates are not known)
fr.	from

front.	frontispiece
fut.	future
fwd.	foreword, foreword by
gen.	general (as in "gen. ed.")
govt.	government
GPO	Government Printing Office, Washington, DC
H. Doc.	House Document
hist.	history, historian, historical
HMSO	Her (His) Majesty's Stationery Office
HR	House of Representatives
H. Rept.	House [of Representatives] Report
H. Res.	House [of Representatives] Resolution
i.e.	*id est* 'that is' (rarely capitalized; set off by commas, unless preceded by a different punctuation mark)
illus.	illustrated by, illustrator, illustration
inc.	incorporated; including
infin.	infinitive
inst.	institute, institution
intl.	international
introd.	(author of) introduction, introduced by, introduction
ips	inches per second (used in reference to recording tapes)
irreg.	irregular
JD	*Juris Doctor* 'Doctor of Law'
jour.	journal
Jr.	Junior
KB	kilobytes
l., ll.	line, lines (avoided in favor of *line* and *lines* or, if clear, numbers only)
lang.	language
LC	Library of Congress
leg.	legal
legis.	legislation, legislative, legislature, legislator
lit.	literally; literary, literature
LLB	*Legum Baccalaureus* 'Bachelor of Laws'
LLD	*Legum Doctor* 'Doctor of Laws'
ltd.	limited
MA	Master of Arts
mag.	magazine

MD	*Medicinae Doctor* 'Doctor of Medicine'
misc.	miscellaneous
MS	Master of Science
ms., mss.	manuscript, manuscripts (the many mss. of Chaucer; Bodleian ms. Tanner 43)
n.	noun
n, nn	note, notes (used immediately after page number: 56n, 56n3, 56nn3–5)
narr.	narrated by, narrator
natl.	national
NB	*nota bene* 'take notice, mark well' (always capitalized)
n.d.	no date (of publication)
NED	*New English Dictionary* (cf. *OED*)
no.	number (cf. *numb.*)
nonstand.	nonstandard
n.p.	no place (of publication); no publisher
n. pag.	no pagination
ns	new series
NS	New Style (calendar)
numb.	numbered
obj.	object, objective
obs.	obsolete
OED	*Oxford English Dictionary* (formerly *New English Dictionary* [*NED*])
op.	opus (work)
orch.	orchestra, orchestrated by
orig.	original, originally
os	old series; original series
OS	Old Style (calendar)
P	Press (used in documentation; see *UP*)
p., pp.	page, pages (omitted before page numbers unless necessary for clarity)
par.	paragraph
part.	participle
perf.	performer, performed by
PhD	*Philosophiae Doctor* 'Doctor of Philosophy'
philol.	philological
philos.	philosophical
pl.	plate; plural
poss.	possessive

pref.	preface, preface by
prep.	preposition
pres.	present
proc.	proceedings
prod.	produced by, producer
pron.	pronoun
pronunc.	pronunciation
PS	postscript
pseud.	pseudonym
pt.	part
pub. (publ.)	published by, publisher, publication
qtd.	quoted
r.	reigned
rec.	recorded, record
reg.	registered; regular
rept.	reported by, report
res.	resolution
resp.	respectively
rev.	revised by, revision; review, reviewed by (spell out *review* where *rev.* might be ambiguous)
rpm	revolutions per minute (used in reference to recordings)
rpt.	reprinted by, reprint
S	Senate
sc.	scene (omitted when act and scene numbers are used together: *Lear* 4.1)
S. Doc.	Senate Document
sec. (sect.)	section
ser.	series
sess.	session
sic	'thus, so' (in square brackets as an editorial interpolation [see 2.6.5], otherwise in parentheses; not followed by an exclamation point)
sing.	singular
soc.	society
Sr.	Senior
S. Rept.	Senate Report
S. Res.	Senate Resolution
st.	stanza
St., Sts. (S, SS)	Saint, Saints
subj.	subject, subjective; subjunctive

substand.	substandard
supp.	supplement
syn.	synonym
trans. (tr.)	translated by, translator, translation; transitive
ts., tss.	typescript, typescripts (cf. *ms.*)
U	University (used in documentation; see *UP*)
UP	University Press (used in documentation: Columbia UP)
usu.	usually
var.	variant
vb.	verb
vers.	version
vol., vols.	volume, volumes
vs. (v.)	versus 'against' (v. preferred in titles of legal cases)
writ.	written by, writer

6.5. Publishers' names

6.5.1. General guidelines

In the list of works cited, shortened forms of publishers' names immediately follow the cities of publication, enabling the reader to locate books or to acquire more information about them. Since publications like *Books in Print*, *Literary Market Place*, and *International Literary Market Place* list publishers' addresses, you need give only enough information so that your reader can look up the publishers in one of these sources. It is usually sufficient, for example, to give *Harcourt* as the publisher's name even if the title page shows *Harcourt Brace Jovanovich* or one of the earlier names of that firm (Harcourt; Harcourt, Brace; Harcourt, Brace, and World). If you are preparing a bibliographical study, however, or if publication history is important to your paper, give the publisher's name in full.

In shortening publishers' names, keep in mind the following:

1. Omit articles, business abbreviations (Co., Corp., Inc., Ltd.), and descriptive words (Books, House, Press, Publishers). When citing a university press, however, always add the abbreviation *P* (Ohio State UP) because

the university itself may publish independently of its press (Ohio State U).

2. If the publisher's name includes the name of one person (Harry N. Abrams, W. W. Norton, John Wiley), cite the surname alone (Abrams, Norton, Wiley). If the publisher's name includes the names of more than one person, cite only the first of these names (Bobbs, Dodd, Faber, Farrar, Funk, Grosset, Harcourt, Harper, Holt, Houghton, McGraw, Prentice, Simon).
3. Use standard abbreviations whenever possible (Acad., Assn., Soc., UP).
4. If the publisher's name is commonly abbreviated with capital initial letters and if the abbreviation is likely to be familiar to your audience, use the abbreviation as the publisher's name (GPO, MLA, UMI). If your readers are not likely to know the abbreviation, shorten the name according to the general guidelines given above (Modern Lang. Assn.).

6.5.2. Selected publishers' names

Acceptable shortened forms of publishers' names include the following:

Abrams	Harry N. Abrams, Inc.
Acad. for Educ. Dev.	Academy for Educational Development, Inc.
ALA	American Library Association
Allen	George Allen and Unwin Publishers, Inc.
Allyn	Allyn and Bacon, Inc.
Appleton	Appleton-Century-Crofts
Ballantine	Ballantine Books, Inc.
Bantam	Bantam Books, Inc.
Barnes	Barnes and Noble Books
Basic	Basic Books
Beacon	Beacon Press, Inc.
Benn	Ernest Benn, Ltd.
Bobbs	The Bobbs-Merrill Co., Inc.
Bowker	R. R. Bowker Co.
CAL	Center for Applied Linguistics
Cambridge UP	Cambridge University Press

Clarendon	Clarendon Press
Columbia UP	Columbia University Press
Cornell UP	Cornell University Press
Dell	Dell Publishing Co., Inc.
Dodd	Dodd, Mead, and Co.
Doubleday	Doubleday and Co., Inc.
Dover	Dover Publications, Inc.
Dutton	E. P. Dutton, Inc.
Einaudi	Giulio Einaudi Editore
Farrar	Farrar, Straus, and Giroux, Inc.
Feminist	The Feminist Press at the City University of New York
Free	The Free Press
Funk	Funk and Wagnalls, Inc.
Gale	Gale Research Co.
Gerig	Gerig Verlag
GPO	Government Printing Office
Harcourt	Harcourt Brace Jovanovich, Inc.
Harper	Harper and Row Publishers, Inc.
Harvard Law Rev. Assn.	Harvard Law Review Association
Harvard UP	Harvard University Press
Heath	D. C. Heath and Co.
HMSO	Her (His) Majesty's Stationery Office
Holt	Holt, Rinehart, and Winston, Inc.
Houghton	Houghton Mifflin Co.
Humanities	Humanities Press, Inc.
Indiana UP	Indiana University Press
Johns Hopkins UP	The Johns Hopkins University Press
Knopf	Alfred A. Knopf, Inc.
Larousse	Librairie Larousse
Lippincott	J. B. Lippincott Co.
Little	Little, Brown, and Co.
Macmillan	Macmillan Publishing Co., Inc.
McGraw	McGraw-Hill, Inc.
MIT P	The MIT Press
MLA	The Modern Language Association of America
NAL	The New American Library, Inc.
NCTE	The National Council of Teachers of English
NEA	The National Education Association

New York Graphic Soc.	New York Graphic Society
Norton	W. W. Norton and Co., Inc.
Oxford UP	Oxford University Press, Inc.
Penguin	Penguin Books, Inc.
Pocket	Pocket Books
Popular	The Popular Press
Prentice	Prentice-Hall, Inc.
Princeton UP	Princeton University Press
PUF	Presses universitaires de France
Putnam's	G. P. Putnam's Sons
Rand	Rand McNally and Co.
Random	Random House, Inc.
Rizzoli	Rizzoli Editore
St. Martin's	St. Martin's Press, Inc.
Scott	Scott, Foresman, and Co.
Scribner's	Charles Scribner's Sons
Simon	Simon and Schuster, Inc.
State U of New York P	State University of New York Press
UMI	University Microfilms International
U of Chicago P	University of Chicago Press
U of Toronto P	University of Toronto Press
UP of Florida	The University Presses of Florida
Viking	The Viking Press, Inc.
Yale UP	Yale University Press

6.6. Symbols and abbreviations used in proofreading and correction

6.6.1. Selected proofreading symbols

The symbols below are used in proofreading typeset material. Many instructors use them in correcting student papers.

Apostrophe or single quotation mark
Close up (basket ball)
Comma
Delete
Insert

¶ Begin a new paragraph
No¶ Do not begin a new paragraph
⊙ Period
“ ” Double quotation marks
Space
∿ Transpose elements, usually with *tr* in margin (thier)

6.6.2. Common correction symbols and abbreviations

Ab	Faulty abbreviation
Adj	Improper use of adjective
Adv	Improper use of adverb
Agr	Faulty agreement
Amb	Ambiguous
Awk	Awkward expression or construction
Cap	Faulty capitalization
D	Faulty diction
Dgl	Dangling construction
Frag	Fragment
lc	Use lowercase
Num	Error in use of numbers
||	Lack of parallelism
P	Faulty punctuation
Ref	Unclear pronoun reference
Rep	Unnecessary repetition
R-O	Run-on
Sp	Error in spelling
SS	Faulty sentence structure
T	Wrong tense of verb
tr	Transpose elements
V	Wrong verb form
Wdy	Wordy

6.7. Literary and religious works

The following abbreviations are examples of those you may use in documentation; it is usually best to introduce the abbreviation in parentheses immediately after the first use of the full title in the text: "In *Paradise Lost* (*PL*), Milton. . . ." For works not on these lists, you may use the abbreviations you find in your sources or devise simple, unambiguous abbreviations of your own.

6.7.1. Bible (Bib.)

The following abbreviations and spelled forms are commonly used for parts of the Bible.

Old Testament (OT)

Gen.	Genesis
Exod.	Exodus
Lev.	Leviticus
Num.	Numbers
Deut.	Deuteronomy
Josh.	Joshua
Judg.	Judges
Ruth	Ruth
1 Sam.	1 Samuel
2 Sam.	2 Samuel
1 Kings	1 Kings
2 Kings	2 Kings
1 Chron.	1 Chronicles
2 Chron.	2 Chronicles
Ezra	Ezra
Neh.	Nehemiah
Esth.	Esther
Job	Job
Ps.	Psalms
Prov.	Proverbs
Eccles.	Ecclesiastes
Song Sol. (also Cant.)	Song of Solomon (also Canticles)
Isa.	Isaiah
Jer.	Jeremiah
Lam.	Lamentations
Ezek.	Ezekiel

Dan.	Daniel
Hos.	Hosea
Joel	Joel
Amos	Amos
Obad.	Obadiah
Jon.	Jonah
Mic.	Micah
Nah.	Nahum
Hab.	Habakkuk
Zeph.	Zephaniah
Hag.	Haggai
Zech.	Zechariah
Mal.	Malachi

Selected Apocryphal and deuterocanonical works

1 Esd.	1 Esdras
2 Esd.	2 Esdras
Tob.	Tobit
Jth.	Judith
Esth. (Apocr.)	Esther (Apocrypha)
Wisd. Sol. (also Wisd.)	Wisdom of Solomon (also Wisdom)
Ecclus. (also Sir.)	Ecclesiasticus (also Sirach)
Bar.	Baruch
Song 3 Childr.	Song of the Three Children
Sus.	Susanna
Bel and Dr.	Bel and the Dragon
Pr. Man.	Prayer of Manasseh
1 Macc.	1 Maccabees
2 Macc.	2 Maccabees

New Testament (NT)

Matt.	Matthew
Mark	Mark
Luke	Luke

John	John
Acts	Acts
Rom.	Romans
1 Cor.	1 Corinthians
2 Cor.	2 Corinthians
Gal.	Galatians
Eph.	Ephesians
Phil.	Philippians
Col.	Colossians
1 Thess.	1 Thessalonians
2 Thess.	2 Thessalonians
1 Tim.	1 Timothy
2 Tim.	2 Timothy
Tit.	Titus
Philem.	Philemon
Heb.	Hebrews
Jas.	James
1 Pet.	1 Peter
2 Pet.	2 Peter
1 John	1 John
2 John	2 John
3 John	3 John
Jude	Jude
Rev. (also Apoc.)	Revelation (also Apocalypse)

Selected Apocryphal works

G. Thom.	Gospel of Thomas
G. Heb.	Gospel of the Hebrews
G. Pet.	Gospel of Peter

6.7.2. Shakespeare

Ado	*Much Ado about Nothing*
Ant.	*Antony and Cleopatra*
AWW	*All's Well That Ends Well*
AYL	*As You Like It*
Cor.	*Coriolanus*

Cym.	*Cymbeline*
Err.	*The Comedy of Errors*
F1	First Folio ed. (1623)
F2	Second Folio ed. (1632)
Ham.	*Hamlet*
1H4	*Henry IV, Part 1*
2H4	*Henry IV, Part 2*
H5	*Henry V*
1H6	*Henry VI, Part 1*
2H6	*Henry VI, Part 2*
3H6	*Henry VI, Part 3*
H8	*Henry VIII*
JC	*Julius Caesar*
Jn.	*King John*
LC	*A Lover's Complaint*
LLL	*Love's Labour's Lost*
Lr.	*King Lear*
Luc.	*The Rape of Lucrece*
Mac.	*Macbeth*
MM	*Measure for Measure*
MND	*A Midsummer Night's Dream*
MV	*The Merchant of Venice*
Oth.	*Othello*
Per.	*Pericles*
PhT	*The Phoenix and the Turtle*
PP	*The Passionate Pilgrim*
Q	Quarto ed.
R2	*Richard II*
R3	*Richard III*
Rom.	*Romeo and Juliet*
Shr.	*The Taming of the Shrew*
Son.	*Sonnets*
TGV	*The Two Gentlemen of Verona*
Tim.	*Timon of Athens*
Tit.	*Titus Andronicus*
Tmp.	*The Tempest*
TN	*Twelfth Night*
TNK	*The Two Noble Kinsmen*
Tro.	*Troilus and Cressida*
Ven.	*Venus and Adonis*
Wiv.	*The Merry Wives of Windsor*
WT	*The Winter's Tale*

6.7.3. Chaucer

CkT	The Cook's Tale
ClT	The Clerk's Tale
CT	*The Canterbury Tales*
CYT	The Canon's Yeoman's Tale
FranT	The Franklin's Tale
FrT	The Friar's Tale
GP	The General Prologue
KnT	The Knight's Tale
ManT	The Manciple's Tale
Mel	The Tale of Melibee
MerT	The Merchant's Tale
MilT	The Miller's Tale
MkT	The Monk's Tale
MLT	The Man of Law's Tale
NPT	The Nun's Priest's Tale
PardT	The Pardoner's Tale
ParsT	The Parson's Tale
PhyT	The Physician's Tale
PrT	The Prioress's Tale
Ret	Chaucer's Retraction
RvT	The Reeve's Tale
ShT	The Shipman's Tale
SNT	The Second Nun's Tale
SqT	The Squire's Tale
SumT	The Summoner's Tale
Th	The Tale of Sir Thopas
WBT	The Wife of Bath's Tale

6.7.4. Other literary works

Aen.	Vergil, *Aeneid*
Ag.	Aeschylus, *Agamemnon*
Ant.	Sophocles, *Antigone*
Bac.	Euripides, *Bacchae*
Beo.	*Beowulf*
Can.	Voltaire, *Candide*
Dec.	Boccaccio, *Decamerone*
DJ	Byron, *Don Juan*

DQ	Cervantes, *Don Quixote*
Eum.	Aeschylus, *Eumenides*
FQ	Spenser, *Faerie Queene*
Gil.	Epic of Gilgamesh
GT	Swift, *Gulliver's Travels*
Hept.	Marguerite de Navarre, *Heptaméron*
Hip.	Euripides, *Hippolytus*
Il.	Homer, *Iliad*
Inf.	Dante, *Inferno*
LB	Wordsworth, *Lyrical Ballads*
Lys.	Aristophanes, *Lysistrata*
MD	Melville, *Moby-Dick*
Med.	Euripides, *Medea*
Mis.	Molière, *Misanthrope*
Nib.	*Nibelungenlied*
Od.	Homer, *Odyssey*
Or.	Aeschylus, *Oresteia*
OR	Sophocles, *Oedipus Rex* (also called *Oedipus Tyrannus* [*OT*])
OT	Sophocles, *Oedipus Tyrannus* (also called *Oedipus Rex* [*OR*])
Par.	Dante, *Paradiso*
PL	Milton, *Paradise Lost*
Prel.	Wordsworth, *Prelude*
Purg.	Dante, *Purgatorio*
Rep.	Plato, *Republic*
SA	Milton, *Samson Agonistes*
SGGK	*Sir Gawain and the Green Knight*
Sym.	Plato, *Symposium*
Tar.	Molière, *Tartuffe*

SAMPLE PAGES OF A RESEARCH PAPER

First page of a research paper

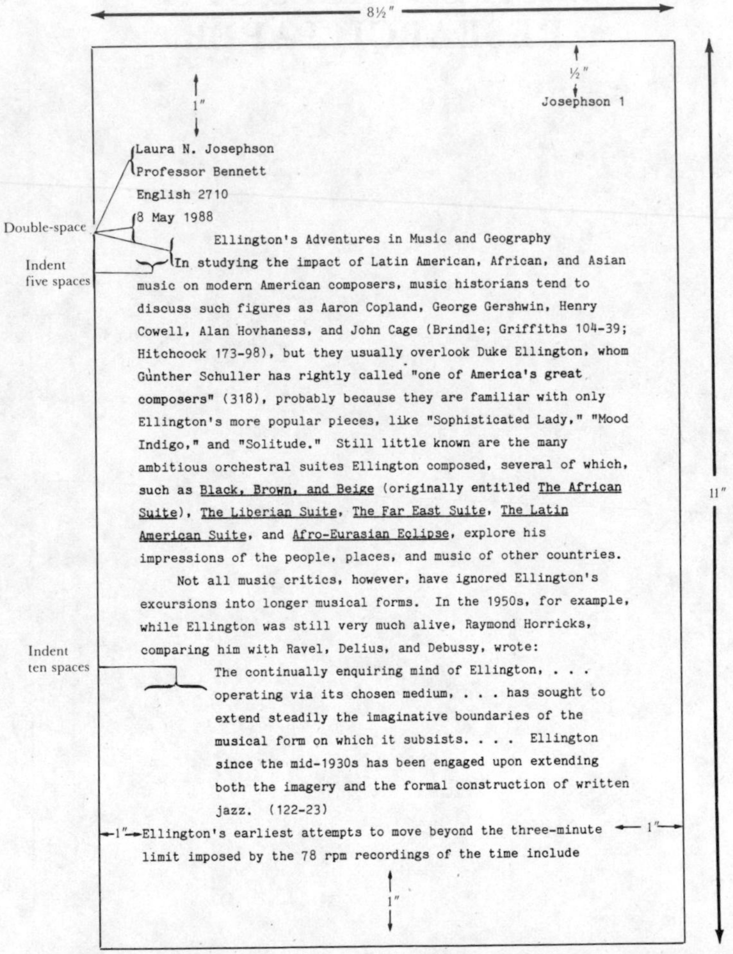

Josephson 1

Laura N. Josephson
Professor Bennett
English 2710
8 May 1988

Ellington's Adventures in Music and Geography

In studying the impact of Latin American, African, and Asian music on modern American composers, music historians tend to discuss such figures as Aaron Copland, George Gershwin, Henry Cowell, Alan Hovhaness, and John Cage (Brindle; Griffiths 104-39; Hitchcock 173-98), but they usually overlook Duke Ellington, whom Günther Schuller has rightly called "one of America's great composers" (318), probably because they are familiar with only Ellington's more popular pieces, like "Sophisticated Lady," "Mood Indigo," and "Solitude." Still little known are the many ambitious orchestral suites Ellington composed, several of which, such as Black, Brown, and Beige (originally entitled The African Suite), The Liberian Suite, The Far East Suite, The Latin American Suite, and Afro-Eurasian Eclipse, explore his impressions of the people, places, and music of other countries.

Not all music critics, however, have ignored Ellington's excursions into longer musical forms. In the 1950s, for example, while Ellington was still very much alive, Raymond Horricks, comparing him with Ravel, Delius, and Debussy, wrote:

> The continually enquiring mind of Ellington, . . . operating via its chosen medium, . . . has sought to extend steadily the imaginative boundaries of the musical form on which it subsists. . . . Ellington since the mid-1930s has been engaged upon extending both the imagery and the formal construction of written jazz. (122-23)

Ellington's earliest attempts to move beyond the three-minute limit imposed by the 78 rpm recordings of the time include

First page of Works Cited

8½″ ½″ 1″ 1″ 1″ 1″ 11″

Josephson 11

Double-space

Works Cited

Brindle, Reginald Smith. "The Search Outwards: The Orient, Jazz, Archaisms." The New Music: The Avant-Garde since 1945. New York: Oxford UP, 1975. 133-45.

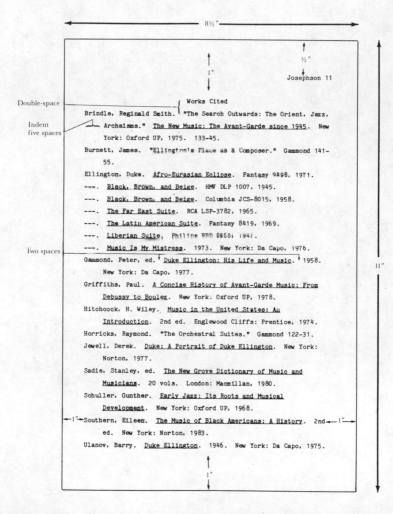

Indent five spaces

Burnett, James. "Ellington's Place as a Composer." Gammond 141-55.

Ellington, Duke. Afro-Eurasian Eclipse. Fantasy 9498, 1971.

---. Black, Brown, and Beige. HMV DLP 1007, 1945.

---. Black, Brown, and Beige. Columbia JCS-8015, 1958.

---. The Far East Suite. RCA LSP-3782, 1965.

---. The Latin American Suite. Fantasy 8419, 1969.

---. Liberian Suite. Philips BBD 0068, 1947.

---. Music Is My Mistress. 1973. New York: Da Capo, 1976.

Two spaces

Gammond, Peter, ed. Duke Ellington: His Life and Music. 1958. New York: Da Capo, 1977.

Griffiths, Paul. A Concise History of Avant-Garde Music: From Debussy to Boulez. New York: Oxford UP, 1978.

Hitchcock, H. Wiley. Music in the United States: An Introduction. 2nd ed. Englewood Cliffs: Prentice, 1974.

Horricks, Raymond. "The Orchestral Suites." Gammond 122-31.

Jewell, Derek. Duke: A Portrait of Duke Ellington. New York: Norton, 1977.

Sadie, Stanley, ed. The New Grove Dictionary of Music and Musicians. 20 vols. London: Macmillan, 1980.

Schuller, Gunther. Early Jazz: Its Roots and Musical Development. New York: Oxford UP, 1968.

Southern, Eileen. The Music of Black Americans: A History. 2nd ed. New York: Norton, 1983.

Ulanov, Barry. Duke Ellington. 1946. New York: Da Capo, 1975.

INDEX